KU-699-012

Preface

This report on CONLAN is directed primarily at toolmakers or developers of software for computer aided design of digital systems, which are familiar with specification and implementation techniques for hardware description and programming languages, rather than at the tool user, i.e. hardware designer, himself.

Every effort has been made to eliminate mistakes and ambiguities from the text. The chairman is indebted to Mssrs. K. Hahn and B. Kreling for their careful review of the manuscript. Many improvements are due to them.

Nevertheless the authors are aware that, due to time pressure and to the difficulties of coordinating the work of an international working group spread over two continents, the present version may still lack conciseness in some parts and sufficient illustrating examples in others.

In spite of possible deficiencies in these areas, it was felt that the report should be published as it stands to get exposure to public reaction as early as possible. This is expected to lead to improvements to be incorporated in a final version and in the CONLAN support software which is presently under development.

During this review period it is planned to publish complementing material on informal explanations of CONLAN features, on examples of language definition and application, and on the support software.

R. Piloty
(Chairman, CONLAN Working Group)

ANDERSONIAN LIBRARY
★
WITHDRAWN
FROM
LIBRARY
STOCK
★
UNIVERSITY OF STRATHCLYDE

WITHDRAWN
FROM
LIBRARY
STOCK

Table of Contents

List of Tables

List of Figures

I Introduction and General Philosophy

1. An Introduction to CONLAN

CONLAN is short for CONsensus LANguage, more specifically, a consensus hardware description language. This report is intended to serve as a self-contained complete description of CONLAN as it stands at the time of publication. The purpose of this part of this report is to provide an informal introduction to CONLAN. Reading part I first will enhance both understanding and appreciation of the formal presentation in parts II, III and IV which set forth the semantics of the CONLAN language. Part V presents the syntax of the language.

1.1. Historical Introduction

The CONLAN project began in 1973 as an attempt to consolidate existing hardware description languages into a standard language. To this end a series of mail ballots were distributed and collected by Dr. G. J. Lipovski, chairman of the Conference on Digital Hardware Languages (CDHL). In September, 1975, a new approach began with the formation of a working group consisting of Dominique Borrione, Yaohan Chu, Donald Dietmeyer, Fredrick Hill, Patrick Skelly, and chaired by Robert Piloty. The Working Group has met at approximately six month intervals in Ottawa, Valley Forge, Toronto, Tucson, Huntsville, Grenoble, Pittsburgh, Palo Alto, Darmstadt, and Anaheim. After the first three meetings, Professor Chu was unable to continue and was replaced by Dr. Barbacci. First results of the Working Group have been reported in [1,2,3,4,5].

Support has been provided by Bell Northern Research, Sperry Univac, Office of Naval Research, Ballistic Missile Defense Advanced Technical Center, Institut National pour la Recherche en Informatique et Automatique, Bundesministerium fur Forschung und Technologie, Siemens, and Fujitsu. Additional support was provided by the author's institutions. The opinions expressed in this report are those of the CONLAN Working group and do not necessarily reflect those of the sponsoring organizations.

1.2. Motivation and Objectives

The decision to start the CONLAN project was motivated by the following assessment of the situation in the area of HDL and of Computer Aided Design (CAD) tools based on them. Several dozens HDL's existed in 1973 [6] and every year since new languages have been proposed and published, mostly from persons in academic institutions [7,8,9]. This tendency to proliferation is in sharp contrast to acceptance in industry. Neither have they been used to document the design process of digital systems nor to support tools for certification, synthesis, and performance evaluation to any appreciable extent. Most CAD tools in industry are designed to aid the manufacturing process (placement, routing, mask layout etc.). The process of systems and logic design is mostly carried out in the traditional way of drawing block and circuit diagrams at the IC package or gate level. In many cases these diagrams are the only true and complete documentation of the system. Most other aspects or phases of the system design, particularly system behaviour, are informally and incompletely described. Simulation as a means for advanced certification is used, if at all, at a very low level (mostly gate level) and hence at enormous cost for more complex systems. Most of the certification is done very late at the level of a physical prototype causing costly changes in physical design.

This situation has not changed very much in the years of CONLAN development: HDL's continue to proliferate [10,11], but their usage in real life design has not increased in the same proportion. Only recently a growing interest in efficient tools for design support at systems and logic level can be observed, probably due to the advance of LSI and VLSI, where late changes make a system more and more costly, and due to increased system complexity in a competive market, calling for more efficient design tools [12,13].

There are several reasons why acceptance of existing HDL's is so low:

1. None of the languages alone is of sufficient scope to portray all aspects of a system and cover all phases of the design process.

2. Languages of different scope are syntactically and semantically unrelated.

3. Few of the languages are formally defined.

4. Only a few languages are implemented.

5. Descriptions are represented by character strings rather than diagrams.

6. There exists no comprehensive hardware and firmware design methodology telling how to use HDL's effectively.

The main aim of the CONLAN Working Group is to remedy the first four deficiencies [14]. Its primary objectives are:

1. To provide a common formal syntactic and semantic base for all levels and aspects of hardware and firmware description, in particular, for descriptions of system structure and behavior.

2. To provide a means for the derivation of user languages from this common base:

   • having a limited scope adjusted to a particular class of design tasks,

   • thus being easy to learn and simple to handle,

   • yet having a well-defined semantic relation among each other.

3. To support CAD tools for documentation, certification, design space exploration, synthesis and so on.

4. To avoid imposing a single rigid style of hardware description on makers of design tools.

The above objectives for a consensus hardware description language call for a language capable of representing hardware at several distinct levels of abstraction. At the lowest level, in which even flip-flops are nonprimitive, gate networks must be described in CONLAN. In contrast, algorithms provide very abstract models of hardware that must interact with lower level hardware descriptions. Thus, these higher level representations must also be expressible in CONLAN. Since the number of levels and the boundaries of each are not universally accepted, CONLAN must be viable for any reasonable set of boundaries.

1.3. The CONLAN Approach

The requirements of this range of language levels suggest not a single consensus language but a family of related languages, languages with consistent syntax and semantics for similar object types and operations. This family should be extensible since all members cannot be prepared simultaneously, indeed all potential members cannot be envisioned at any point in time. That family members be consistent requires that extensibility be controlled.

CONLAN addresses these fundamental requirements by supporting a self-defining, extensible family of languages. Its member languages are tied together by a common core syntax and a common semantic definition system. The CONLAN construct to define a member language is called a language definition segment. Each new language definition segment is based upon an existing one, its reference language, to enhance consistency and increase language definition efficiency. Member languages are also used to write descriptions of hardware, firmware or software modules, of course. Description definition segments are provided for this purpose.

The CONLAN family of languages is open ended. New languages may be derived from existing ones at any given point in time as the need arises. These in turn may be used later as reference languages for further languages.

The same construction mechanism and the same notational system used to provide descriptions are also used to define new language members. In this sense CONLAN is self-defining in contrast to externally defined languages using a separate language to define its semantics, e.g. the formal description of PL/I using the Vienna Definition Language [15].

To initialize the CONLAN family the CONLAN Working Group has prepared the root language called Base CONLAN (bcl) as the interface between the CONLAN Working Group and its public. Bcl provides a carefully chosen set of basic objects reflecting the CONLAN concept of time and space, of signals and carriers, of arrays and records. These concepts are expected to prevail throughout the family. To test and illustrate the language construction mechanism a very low level but powerful language called Primitive Set CONLAN (pscl) was used to formally define bcl. pscl has no parent language. It owns a set of primitive objects whose domains and operations are introduced informally.

Base CONLAN is primarily a starting point, with well defined and semantically sound primitives, for language designers to derive a coherent and comprehensive family of computer hardware description languages. As a result, hardware descriptions written in Base CONLAN may look verbose. Nevertheless, all concepts pertinent to hardware modeling are already in Base CONLAN and may be common to all languages of the CONLAN family.

2. CONLAN Concepts

The purpose of this informal narrative is to prepare the reader for the formal portions of this report and to focus attention on the more significant aspects of CONLAN. Parts II to V of this report are the complete definition of CONLAN and no attempt will be made to repeat its exhaustive treatment in this introduction. In fact, details and examples will be avoided here. Many concepts and notational conventions of existing programming and hardware description languages will be found in CONLAN. To some extent decisions to include or exclude such concepts and conventions will be justified; clearly all details of years of group research and debate cannot and should not be fully reported.

2.1. Segments, statements

The basic ideas of structured programming were considered to be also valid for hardware description languages. As a consequence, valid CONLAN text consists of properly nested blocks. Blocks which define an entity, either a language item or a hardware module, are called segments. Blocks that refer to or invoke an instance of a segment are called statements. Bodies of segments typically consist of statements. Segments begin with a keyword followed by an identifier 'and terminate with keyword END which may, but need not be followed by the segment identifier. Most statements begin with a keyword and terminate with END which may be followed by the opening keyword. These concepts are not new; their familiarity should put the reader at ease.

However there are two basic differences with respect to programming languages:

- total concurrency

- structure description

These differences are discussed in the following.

2.2. Concurrency

In CONLAN there is no implied or explicit division between data structure and control structure in describing behaviour by operation invocation. Lists of operation invocations in CONLAN do not imply a sequence of execution. Also there are no sequencing operations, like goto, provided as primitives. All invocations of operations are potentially executed concurrently, at least within the scope of one block. Conditional invocations of operations (IF and CASE statements), however, permit time selection of operation execution by specifying conditions on the system state under which an operation is supposed to be executed.

The most basic form for behaviour description in CONLAN is concurrent execution of connections between terminals (i.e., specification of signal flow) in a network. Higher forms of behaviour descriptions, e.g., in terms of conditional assignment of values to abstract variables or of time attributed setting and resetting of flipflops or of loading registers, are provided or may be constructed from Base Conlan.

2.3. Structure Description versus Behaviour Description

Similar to procedure declarations in programming languages CONLAN provides operation definition segments, which serve to specify a new operation for later invocation in a behaviour description.

In addition, however, CONLAN provides similar to some existing hardware description languages [16], description definition segments to specify hardware module types, a construct not normally present in programming languages. Description segments serve to describe the structure of hardware by nested instantiation of predefined module types. Thereby, a particular module type may be either described in terms of submodules, i.e. instances of some other module types (structure description), or in terms of operation invocations (behaviour description). Consequently at every level of operational abstraction, CONLAN allows its user the choice of structural or behavioural description or both in mixed form (e.g., data path structurally, control part behaviourally).

2.4. Language and Description Definition Segments

We explore CONLAN by its types of segments. The language definition segment (keyword CONLAN) defines a new member of the CONLAN family. The description definition segment (keyword DESCRIPTION) defines a hardware or firmware system. To a large extent different groups of people are expected to write these two types of segments. Those who prepare new members of the CONLAN family and software to support their new members will be referred to as toolmakers; those who use those new languages and supporting software to record their hardware design efforts are users. In many organizations toolmakers are members of the Design Automation Department and users are members of Engineering Design Departments. A toolmaker writes a CONLAN segment; a user writes a DESCRIPTION. The outermost segment in both cases must be prefaced with a reference language statement (keyword REFLAN). The existing (reference) language revealed in the REFLAN statement provides the syntax and semantics immediately available for use in writing the body of the outermost segment. A new language is said to be derived from its reference language. All members of the CONLAN family are derived from bcl, possibly through a long chain of intermediate languages.

Several methods for hiding portions of a language from users and future toolmakers are available in CONLAN:

- First, segments marked PRIVATE are neither visible nor accessible to future tookmakers and users.

- Second, identifiers and keywords that terminate with the symbol @ are not visible to users.

- Third, while nonPRIVATE segments of a reference language provide objects and operations for a toolmaker to be used in writing a CONLAN segment to define a new language, those objects and operations are not automatically available to users of the new language and future toolmakers. Redefinition of segments to be propagated from the reference to the new language is avoided by the CARRY statement in which segments to be propagated are revealed. Keyword CARRYALL may replace the CARRY statement in a special, obvious case. Further, EXTERNAL segments may be used to avoid repetitive writing of the same CONLAN text. EXTERNAL statements stand in place of the original segment definition, just as though that original segment were copied at the point of the EXTERNAL segment.

- Fourth, hiding and preventing language features from appearing in derived languages may also be accomplished by syntax modification statements (keyword FORMAT@), which will be discussed in a subsequent section.

The hiding mechanisms described above permit toolmakers to prepare simple hardware description languages for specific application areas while maintaining a clear semantic and syntatic relation with their ancestor languages.

To summarize, the CONLAN text structure is shown in Figure 2-1. At any given point in time it consists of a set of language definition segments and a set of description segments. Each segment is under the scope of a REFLAN statement. In a language definition segment this statement points to the language from which the new language is directly derived. Thus language la11 is directly derived from la1, and la21 is directly derived from la2. In a description segment the REFLAN statement points to the language in which the description is written.

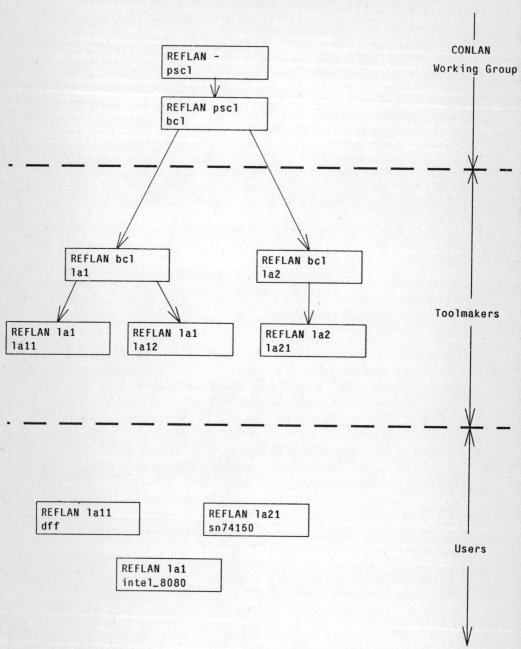

Figure 2-1: CONLAN text structure

2.5. Type and Operation Definition Segments

pscl provides the fundamental objects of the CONLAN family; bcl provides more elaborate objects that are expected to be useful for hardware description throughout the CONLAN family. Other members of the CONLAN family are expected to provide additional hardware and firmware items as objects. Objects are usually collected into sets that may or may not be explicitly named. All objects are members of at least one universal set, named univ@, provided by pscl. The CONLAN method for language construction and hence semantic definition is based upon the concept of abstract data types as developed for programming languages CLU [17] and ALPHARD [18].

A CONLAN object type, or simply type, consists of a set of objects (its domain) together with operations defined on the members of that set. The operations however are defined explicitly in terms of operations already defined, particularly in terms of operations provided by the reference language (Operationally defined data types). The TYPE segment provides a means for specifying the set membership and defining the operations of the defined type. The name of the TYPE segment is used as the name of the domain as well as the set of operations available in it, depending on the context. A TYPE segment may be parameterized. Such definitions provide a family of types. A member of the family is obtained by binding the formal parameters to actual parameters. The name of the type segment, possibly followed by a list of actual parameters, is a type designator (e.g., array(bool)).

As may be expected, TYPE segments within a CONLAN or DESCRIPTION segment may be written in terms of the nonPRIVATE types of the reference language. In addition, TYPE segments may be written in terms of previously written TYPE segments. In particular, the domain of a new type is always defined as the subset of the domain of exactly one previously defined type, its parent or defining type. The operation of the parent type may be used to define the operations of the new type. However, they are no longer applicable to the elements of the new type. This process is called type derivation. It leads to a tree-structure of the types of a language, just as the reference language provides a tree-structure on the members of the CONLAN family.

Subtypes may be derived from existing types using a SUBTYPE segment. Their domain is a subset of the domain of their parent type. They inherit automatically all operations of the parent type. During type checking subtypes are considered compatible with their parent type.

Experience with programming languages has revealed the value of requiring users of a language to specify the set of which each referenced object is a member, i.e., to specify the type of all identifiers used. While hardware description languages have not provided traditional data types (integer, real, complex, etc.), many have introduced hardware types (register, terminal, clock, etc.). Objects that are able to hold other objects are known as carriers . pscl provides the basic carrier type, called "cell@" and operations on them. To gain error checking capability CONLAN requires the type of all objects to be specified. This permits the check of type compatibility between formal and actual parameters (type checking). Normally identity of types is required for compatibility. Exceptions are subtypes and standard dereferencing rules between carrier types and their content types.

When all operations on an existing type or type family are desired on a subset of that parent type or a member of that parent type family, repetitive definition is avoided with the concise SUBTYPE segment which permits no new operations to be introduced.

On occasion it is necessary for toolmakers to group together types with a common property. A set of such types is a class. Members of a class are thus types, and not objects of the grouped types. One class that contains all types is provided by pscl. It is named any@ . New classes may be derived from any@ using the CLASS segment. Type families implicitly define classes consisting of the family members.

A great deal of time and effort has gone into precisely defining many things that are often taken as "known" in programming and hardware description languages. "Operation" is an example. Briefly, CONLAN admits two categories of operations. First, an operation is a formal rule for selecting one or more "result" objects from designated result types. This corresponds to the mathematical "function". Second, an operation is the selection of one or more result objects and their placement in a carrier. They are called "activities".

New operations are defined with FUNCTION and ACTIVITY segments. The FUNCTION segment defines an operation that selects and returns an element of a specified type. "Return" is another of those "known" concepts and the CONLAN definition is consistent with the usual notion. The ACTIVITY segment defines an operation that does not return objects. Thus identifiers of ACTIVITY segments may not appear in expressions. Activities parallel procedures and subroutines of programming languages in this respect.

CONLAN text, like text of all formal languages, has significance only if it is read and responded to by a person or machine (an environment) and then only to the extent that the environment reads and responds in a well defined manner. Many pages of this report are devoted to specifying the manner in which CONLAN text is to be read if logic simulation is intended. But not all such rules can be written in advance for all future members of the CONLAN family, not all applications of CONLAN text can be anticipated, and some responses are not appropriately specified via CONLAN text but best left to software toolmakers, e.g., response to error conditions. FUNCTION and ACTIVITY segments may be prefixed with keyword INTERPRETER@ to indicate that the defined operations are to be invoked by the environment of the CONLAN member of which the operations are a part. A comment indicates when it should be invoked. The environment is expected to call upon such operations appropriately; this is the responsibility of the software toolmaker. Users may not write such operations, of course, and should seldom be aware that they exist in the CONLAN member languages they use.

2.6. Identifiers, Parameters and Interface Carriers

CONLAN utilizes the international standard ISO 646 character set and code which is designated a the International Reference Version (IRV). The semantics of most symbols of that set have been determined by the Working Group. Toolmakers may assign semantics to a few remaining symbols and to concatenations of symbols (compound symbols). Members of the upper case are called capitals; members of the lower case are letters. It should be obvious by now that keywords are sequences of capitals possibly terminated by symbol '@'. CONLAN text destined for publication where a richer character set is available may utilize a limited set of specified substitutions for the ISO 646-IRV characters, and different typefaces.

CONLAN deals with the following categories of entities:

- Objects

- Operations

- Types

- Classes

- Descriptions and Instances of Descriptions

- Languages

Identifiers are most often used to denote CONLAN objects. Simple identifiers start with at least one letter followed by an arbitrary string of letters, digits, and underscore ('_'), of any length and terminating with a letter, or digit, or with the symbol '@'. While software may impose a length limitation on identifiers, in principle identifiers may be very descriptive words or sequences of words separated by underscores. Contiguous underscores are prohibited in CONLAN to emphasize their intended use as separators for mnemonic constituents of simple identifiers (e.g. address_reg). The symbol '@' denotes a system identifier which may be used only within a language definition segment. Compound identifiers are two or more simple identifiers separated by periods ('.'). They permit one to prefix a simple identifier with one or more enclosing segment identifiers when the corresponding object is referenced outside the segment providing the simple identifier.

Objects are the operands for CONLAN operations. While identifiers may always stand in their place, constant denotations are available for identifying specific elements of many CONLAN types. We will see constant denotations when we preview pscl.

Formal and actual parameters in CONLAN are as in most languages. A formal parameter is denoted by an identifier representing any element of a given type. Formal parameters appearing in a parameter list of an operation, type, or description must be typed; i.e., the parameter must be followed by the designator of the type of which the parameter is a element separated by a colon (e.g., x: bool). The type designator (bool) defines the domain of x and the operations applicable to it. This requirement facilitates checking: When a formal parameter is bound to an actual parameter, its associated type designator is used to check if the type of the actual parameter is equivalent to the type of the formal parameter. The type of the actual parameter is normally explicitly stated in a declaration, or in one of the constructs involving predicates (yet to be discussed). If the actual parameter is a constant denotation, it can also be checked to determine that it belongs to the domain of the prescribed type. The binding of actual to formal parameters and the importing and exporting of information from segments are discussed in great detail in part II.

CONLAN operations are normally denoted by an identifier prefixing a list of parameters (operands). Operator symbols may be introduced via syntax modification for prefix and infix notation, either in lieu of a standard functional notation or as an alternative to it.

The typed identifiers enclosed in parentheses following the identifier of a DESCRIPTION segment are seldom parameters in the conventional sense. Attributes may appear; if they do, a family of descriptions is defined. Such parameters are treated quite differently from the other entries, the interface carriers. In addition to being typed, interface carriers are tagged to indicate the direction of information flow that they support. They provide all communication between the inside of the description and its environment, just as all communication with an encapsulated hardware module (e.g., an IC) must be via its pins.

2.7. Statements
While the intent of the CARRY, EXTERNAL and REFLAN statements has already been revealed, many CONLAN statements remain to be discussed. A predicate is any expression that produces a Boolean result. The first statements to be discussed are forms of predicates. FORALL@, FORSOME@ and FORONE@ statements test the domain of a type against an embedded predicate and evaluate to true (1 in CONLAN) or false (0) as the keywords suggest.

The THE@ statement selects the one element of the domain of the type for which an embedded predicate is true. The ALL statement selects all elements for which an embedded predicate is true; it constructs a subset and is particularily useful in writing TYPE segments. Since users may have occasion to write such segments the ALL keyword is not restricted by a terminal @ symbol.

The IF and CASE statements selectively invoke one of a list of operations based upon the value of a predicate or predicates. Both permit an ELSE part. The IF statement also permits an unlimited number of ELIF (else if) parts.

The OVER statement provides a short way of writing a collection of operation invocations that differ only in the value of an index. The OVER statement is not a loop constructor as found in programming languages where sequence as well as invocation is specified. In fact, provisions for expressing sequential evaluation of invoked ACTIVITY segments are largely absent from pscl and bcl as indicated already in Section 2.2.

The evaluation sequence between several invoked FUNCTION segments is expressed via an operator hierarchy and the use of parentheses. But procedural descriptions of hardware are not possible until a CONLAN member language is written that provides suitable control structures. The Working Group has performed experiments and believes that bcl supports the development of such control structures, and therefore expects to see them in some of the first CONLAN members derived from bcl.

The DECLARE statement provides a means of assigning a name to an element of a specified type or of renaming an already named object. In hardware descriptions the local objects must be declared as we will see. The importance of being able to assign multiple names (naming a subregister) is well known. Further, using names throughout a program or hardware description rather than constant denotations is considered to be good practice. Contrast the DECLARE with the USE statement which assigns a name to an instance of a description, i.e., a module, and implicitly declares the interface carriers of that instance.

The DESCRIPTION segment may be thought to bring an infinite set of identical hardware units into the stockroom. No modules exist in a specific system until one goes to the stockroom, requests a specific number of modules, and assigns a name to each via a USE statement. When the modules are acquired, their interface terminals come with them, and may be identified by a compound name involving the name assigned to the module of which they are a part. We see more clearly the CONLAN distinction between an operation and a description.

The FORMAT@ statement provides the toolmaker with a means of deriving the syntax of a new language from the syntax of its reference language. Productions may be modified and given additional semantic meaning with the FORMAT@ statement, but not without limit. A system of rights on productions establishes the limits. The presence of one type of right indicates that the production or alternative can be removed in a future CONLAN segment, but the name of the non-terminal cannot be used for a new production, i.e., it can be deleted but not replaced. The presence of a second type of right on a production indicates that alternatives may be added to the production. The absence of all such rights indicates that the production or alternative may not be altered in any way. By carefully placing rights on the bcl grammar the Working Group intends to ensure the consistency of all CONLAN member languages while permitting toolmakers to keep the syntax of a new language as simple as possible and yet incorporate new constructs to denote specific features such as an infix symbol for a new, important operation. The set of productions that may never be deleted, and thus is common to all CONLAN members is the core syntax.

The @ on keyword FORMAT@ prevents users from including such statements in their operation definition segments. Toolmakers however, can use FORMAT@ statements to extend their grammars to recognize invocations of the new operation, perhaps with infix symbolism, and extend the semantics of existing productions when the new operator on a new type closely parallels operations on older types.

Finally, the ASSERT statement provides a means for toolmakers and users to specify predicates and other boolean relations between inputs and outputs of operations or descriptions that they expect to be true. It is similar to the notation of "specifications" introduced in [19]. An error condition exists if an assertion proves to be false. While ASSERT statements have not been used extensively in developing bcl from pscl, they are expected to be especially valuable in hardware description. Setup and hold time specifications on flip-flops are naturally checked via assertions, for example. Also size constraints on actual array parameters may be tested using assertions.

3. A Preview of Primitive Set CONLAN (pscl)

CONLAN is built from Primitive Set CONLAN (pscl). pscl is an exceptional member of the CONLAN family in that there is no reference language for pscl, object sets are assumed rather than defined, and operators on objects are assumed rather than being defined in more fundamental terms. The types, classes and operations which are assumed in pscl are previewed in this chapter as well as the pscl model of computation.

3.1. Types, Classes and Operations

Type **int** consists of all integers, together with operations '=', '~=', '<', '=<', '>', '>=', '+', '-', '*', '/', '↑', and 'MOD' provided without formal definition, i.e., they are "known." Integers are mathematical entities; there is no upper limit on the magnitude that may be expressed. Since integers are of great utility in hardware description languages, but not hardware objects, many functions are assumed in int. A standard denotation for signed and unsigned integers in decimal, binary, octal or hexadecimal base is provided by the syntax.

Type **bool** has two members, denoted by 1 and 0 representing "true" and "false" respectively, together with operations '=', '~=', '&', '|', '~', '<', '=<', '>', '>='. A small, but not minimal, set of familiar, basic operations is assumed here and in the types below to ensure the semantics of the majority of hardware oriented operations by requiring that they be implemented. The relational operators are based upon '0' being less than '1'.

Type **string** consists of all sequences of characters, together with operations '=', '~=', '<', '=<', '>', '>=', and **order@**. A string is denoted by enclosing the sequence in single quotes ('). The relational operators are based on the order of characters in the ISO 646 table. Further, function order@ returns an integer that is unique to the string given as a parameter. Another useful order on strings is established through these integers.

Type **cell@(t: any@)** comprises an infinite number of elements each of which may hold at most one element of type t at any point in time. This element is called the cell's content, and may change over time. Cells are therefore the basic carriers of CONLAN. No constant denotation exists for cells. Rather, a name must be associated with a cell via a declaration statement before it can be referenced. Function **empty@(x)** tells if cell x is empty or not. Function **get@(x)** returns the contents of cell x. If the cell x is empty an error condition exists. Activity **put@(x,u)**, the primitive activity of CONLAN, replaces the contents of cell x with u. Cells are modifiable objects in that their contents may change over time. These are the only pscl objects with this attribute and constitute the basis for all modifiable objects in the CONLAN family.

Type **tuple@** consists of all lists of elements of univ@, together with operations '=', '~=', **size@**, **select@**, **remove@**, and **extend@**. Tuple@ includes the empty list and lists having tuples themselves as members (nested tuples). A tuple is denoted via a list of object denotations enclosed in '(' and ')', and separated by commas. Two tuples are equal ('=') if they have the same number of and identical members in identical order. Otherwise they are not equal ('~='). Function size@(x) returns the number of members of a tuple. Consecutive integers from 1 to size@(x) identify the positions of the members of tuple x. Only the positions of this range may be referenced without error. Function select@(x,i) returns the member of tuple x in position i. Function remove@(x,i) returns the tuple consisting of all the members of x except the ith member. Function extend@(x,u) returns the tuple consisting of all the members of x, followed by u as the last member.

Type **univ@** consists of all members of all types defined in any member of the CONLAN family, together with operators '=' and '~='. It permits the present definition of operations on objects to be defined in the future, and is a necessary part of pscl if highly exceptional rules are to be avoided in CONLAN. Type univ@ is considered as the defining type for the other types of pscl, from which all other types of CONLAN will be derived.

Class **any@** is the universal class in CONLAN. Its domain is the set of all types defined in any member of the CONLAN family, together with operations '=', '~=', '.<', '<|' and 'designate@'. Function '.<' ("belongs to") may be used to determine if an object from univ@ is also an element of a defined type (a member of any@). Function '<|' ("derived from") may be used to determine if a member of any@ (a type) was derived from another member of any@ or a specified class. Function 'designate@' will be explained later on in Chapter 2.

Class **carr_type** is the subclass of any@ comprising all carrier types. In pscl, its domain consists of all members of the primitive carrier type family cell@(t) and all types derived from it using pscl as a reference language. All operations applicable to the elements of any@ are also applicable to those of class carr type.

Figure 3-1 clarifies the universal set univ@ and the universal class any@. Since univ@ is a type, it is a member of any@. Those subsets of univ@ that are named via a type definition are also members of any@. Unnamed sets may be created in CONLAN by enumeration of arbitrary elements of univ@; being unnamed they are not members of any@. univ@ and any@ have the same significance to CONLAN as a universal set has to set algebra. They are necessary to place CONLAN on a sound theoretical foundation.

It took the Working Group a great deal of time to refine this minimal collection of types and classes. We believe that is was time well spent, however, and that all useful hardware description types can be derived from this fundamental collection.

3.2. pscl Model of Computation

In addition to the primitive pscl object types and classes (Section 3.1, 13, 14) a model of computation is provided for pscl (Section 15) in order to specify unambiguously the semantics of pscl descriptions (operational semantic definition).

This model specifies the rules for the evaluation of the next state of all carriers involved in a description from their previous state in terms of the operations invoked in that description.

The model views the evaluation of a description as a task to be performed in a mill employing specialized workers for the different computational tasks appearing in the description. A worker is hired for each carrier, instance of description and operation invocation.

A set of messages is available to the workers to intercommunicate during evaluation. Command messages are passed down from the root description worker to the hierarchy of subordinate workers to initiate execution of their task. Done messages are returned by the individual workers upon completion of their task

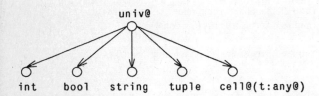

Figure 3-1: Type and class structure of pscl

through the hierarchy of their callers up to the root worker to signal the termination of one pscl evaluation cycle.

4. A Preview of Base Conlan (bcl)

bcl was developed to illustrate and test the language construction mechanism and to provide the types expected to pervade the CONLAN family. While the Working Group has no control over toolmakers, we feel that derived languages are truly 'CONLAN members' if they are derived from bcl, not pscl. We expect toolmakers to adhere to our definitions of arrays, records, signals, carriers, etc...; we remove all justification for repeating the basic task of constructing a language from pscl by providing all the objects that toolmakers require to develop user oriented members of the CONLAN family.

The type derivation tree of bcl is shown in Figure 17-1. A complete discussion of all these types is out of order here, so this chapter will concentrate on motivation for and justification of the bcl types.

4.1. Basic Type Classes

In bcl three basic classes of object types are distinguished:

- value types

- signal types

- carrier types

They are formally defined in Part IV. Reserved identifiers "val_type", "sig_type" and "carr_type" are used as designators.

Value types in bcl are all types derived from the pscl types "int", "bool" and "string" and by enumeration from univ@ (excluding tuples and cells). Their elements are scalar values. Composite value types may be constructed in derived languages using array and record constructors (Section 4.4).

Signal types in bcl are all types derived from members of the bcl type family "signal". Their elements are time sequences of scalar values (Section 4.5).

Carrier types are all types derived from the three basic bcl signal carrier type families "terminal", "variable" and "rtvariable" (real time variable) to be introduced in Section 4.6. Their elements are cells containing signals.

4.2. Value Types

Types **int**, **bool** and **string** are carried as values from pscl. Types **nnint** (nonnegative integers), **pint** (positive integers) and **bint** (bounded integers) are introduced as subtypes of int to be used in the development of bcl.

Boolean operations **nor**, **xor**, **eqv** and **nand** are included to provide users with these desirable operations and to illustrate the writing of free-standing operations in a CONLAN segment, i.e., operations defined outside the scope of a type segment.

Format statements in the boolean function definitions illustrate syntax modification. Whenever multiple instances of the same operator symbol or name are introduced, the types of the operands determine which specific operation is being invoked.

4.3. Typed Tuples

Typed tuples, tuples in which all members are of a specific type, are fundamental to the structured objects developed in bcl such as array, records and signals. The **tytuple@.select@** function is similar to the tuple@.select@ function of pscl, but that function was not carried in order to restrict the type of its result; in doing so the CONLAN subscripting notation, x[.y.] for tytuple@.select@(x,y), could be introduced and used in subsequent definitions. Functions **tytuple@.extend@** similarly introduces the concatenate symbol, '#', of CONLAN; function **tytuple@.catenate@** generalizes the concept. Subtypes **inttuple** and **pinttuple** provide very useful special cases of the typed tuple.

4.4. Arrays and Records

Types **range@**, **array_dimension@** and **indexer@** are defined to support the definitions of arrays, records, and other structured objects of bcl. In brief, a range is a tuple of consecutive, ascending or descending integers. A format statement provides a notation for expressing a range; a colon (:) separates the left and right bounds of the list of integers. Such notation is expected to be used in expressing dimensions of and selecting parts of arrays. An array_dimension is a tuple of ranges. Syntax modification indicates that the ranges are to be separated by semicolons (;). Multi- dimensioned arrays are therefore supported in bcl with a notation that is widely, if not universally used. Indexers are like array dimensions, but they are tuples of more general inttuples where integers are not necessarily consecutive or unique. They are used in the array selection process as opposed to the array declaration process.

In brief, a CONLAN array is a tuple with two members. The first member records the declared subscript range(s) of the array, and therefore provides the form of the array as well. The second member records the objects organized in the one or more dimensioned, rectangular form that usually is termed an array. Users of CONLAN arrays are not necessarily aware of this structure, of course, but the definition of functions on arrays demands that it be carefully defined.

The array functions defined in bcl might well be anticipated. Arrays may be subscripted, transposed and concatenated. In addition, to retain the uniform meaning of '=' and '~=' as given in pscl for type tuple@, additional equality testing functions are defined. Functions **equal** and **not_equal** test two arrays for identical value parts and compatible dimension parts, and functions **eq** and **neq** return arrays in which the equality or nonequality of individual values are expressed. Further, generic operations (with the specific operation given as a parameter) are provided for arrays so that functions, like integer addition to be performed on corresponding objects of arrays with the same dimensionality to form a result array of that dimensionality, need not be redefined on arrays.

Records are structured objects in which the components may be of different types and are referred to by a name, rather than a number as in array subscripting. A select function on records permits one to extract the object in a field of the record; a format statement in the definition of the select function introduces the exclamation mark (!) separating the record and field names as the CONLAN notation for field selection.

4.5. Time and Signals

There is no formal definition of time in pscl. Expressions, including predicates, are part of pscl and the process for evaluation of expressions is postulated as part of that language. 'Before-after' relations are needed in expression evaluation, but no advancement of real time is required. The CONLAN model of time is introduced where it is first required; it is superimposed on CONLAN signals after they are derived from typed tuples.

Real time is broken into uniform durations called intervals identified with integers greater than zero. Ascending, successive integers are associated with contiguous intervals. No relation between the interval and real time (the physical unit "Second") exists in general. An implementation may impose such a relation or permit users to specify such a relation. At the beginning of each interval there are an indefinite number of calculation steps identified with integers greater than zero. Successive steps provide a before-after relation only. Real time does not advance as successive steps are taken.

Users of a low level CONLAN family member, for example, a gate level CONLAN, will have available a variety of activities, some of which will cause real time to advance and some not. They may take advantage of this by using computation steps to accomplish bookkeeping calculations and advancing real time only to model time dependent circuit activity. In higher level CONLAN family members, single interval activities may have disappeared to be replaced by clock-synchronized activities, each invocation of which will cause several real time intervals to elapse. At this level complex calculations will be accomplished over long sequences of computation steps with occasional clock transfers to advance real time. The precise timing interpretations of all activities and functions at any level is formally linked to bcl by activity and function segments.

The environment is assumed to maintain two special objects that support the CONLAN model of time: t@ is an object of type cell@(int) whose value is the current time interval; s@ is an object of type cell@(int) whose value is the current calculation step. Contiguous values are provided in ascending order starting with one in both cases; therefore those objects are referred to as 'counters.' When the environment determines via an evaluation algorithm that it is appropriate, it increments the value provided by t@ and resets the s@ counter to 1.

A computation step signal, cs_signal@(x: any@), is a tuple of elements of type x, where the elements correspond to the results of the last two computation steps. Generic type cs_signal@(x) is normally used with x being bound to some scalar value type, such as int or bool.

Functions of type cs_signal@ permit selecting a value from a computation step signal, extending and reducing such a signal by one value. A format statement introduces the use of braces, { and }, to select with subscript-like notation. This leve of construction is provided for the toolmaker's benefit; users may not use types with an @ in their identifier, and in general will not be aware of the structure of CONLAN signals.

A CONLAN signal, type signal(x: val_type), is a tuple of computation step signals of values of type x with a default value affixed. Each cs_signal@ of a signal corresponds to a value of t@; their order in a signal corresponds to the successive values of t@. A signal then is a tuple of tuples of values.

Functions of type signal permit selecting a constituent cs_signal@ or a value from a cs_signal@, extending a signal by one value, and compacting a signal by eliminating all but the last value from the present (front end) cs_signal. A delay function with delay parameter d may be applied to a signal x, using the format x%d. It returns a signal with all constituent cs_signals shifted d time units toward the present and cs_signals with default values appended during the first d time units.

In addition, functions on signals are provided which are invoked automatically by the bcl environment. They are marked by INTERPRETER@. An example of such a function is val(x) which returns the front end value of signal x. It is invoked whenever a formal parameter of class val_type is bound by an actual parameter of class sig_type.

Computation step signals and signals are tuples and hence may be very large. While the use of such tuples to record complete histories of values is conceptually most appealing to the Working Group, and hopefully other toolmakers and users, very large tuples will not lead to efficient software. The Working Group recognizes this and does not propose that software retain complete histories. It realizes that actual software will only retain history for a fixed period of time depending on the delay properties of the system being described. In general, we do not mean this report to be taken as an indication of how efficient software is to be written, but rather as a specification of the semantics and syntax that efficient software must provide.

4.6. Carriers

bcl carriers are cells containing bcl signals. Three type families of such signal carriers are provided for the user of bcl:

Type family terminal(x: val_type; def: x) represents signal carriers with no retention properties between computation steps or intervals. The first parameter x determines the value type of the signals being held by the carrier, the second determines the default value to be used during execution of its activities.

Activity connect, with infix symbol '.=', places a value given as the right operand of .= in the last position of the current interval of the carrier named as the left operand. If two or more connect activities are invoked on the same terminal during one step, attempting to place different values into it, an error message is generated. But if no connect activity is invoked during a computation step to extend the signal of a terminal, the default value of the terminal is placed in the signal by an interpreter activity. Another interpreter activity introduces a new cs_signal in the signal of each terminal when interval counter t@ is about to be incremented. These activities are named **finstep** and **finint**, respectively. In addition interpreter activities **shrink** and **setlength** are used by the evaluation algorithm to adjust the length of signals in carriers.

Boolean terminals model wires. Some wires float high and others float low when not driven. Subtypes **btm0** and **btm1** are provided with obvious fixed default values so that users are relieved of repeatedly supplying these commonly desired default values. Subtype **btml(default: bool)** permits users to specify a default value for a boolean terminal, should they prefer to do so.

Type family **variable(x: val_type; def: x)** represents signal_carries with retention properties. Activity **assign**, with infix symbol ':=', is provided to extend the signals of variables. If assign is not invoked for a variable during a computation step, the current value is used to extend the signal. Thus a value is carried from step to step when a new value is not provided. Variables are therefore much as found in programming languages. Boolean variables may be thought to model idealized latches. Subtypes **bvar(init:bool)** and **ivar(init:int)** are provided so that users need supply only initial values for boolean and integer variables.

Type **rtvariable(x: val_type; def: x)** represents real time variables modelling idealized, unit delay flip-flops. Activity **transfer**, with infix symbol '<-', may be invoked to place a value in a new cs_signal of the signal of a rtvariable. Appropriate interpreter activities finstep, finint, shrink and setlength are defined for variables and rt_variables also.

4.7. The bcl Model of Computation

The model of computation (Section 19) for the evaluation of a description written in bcl consists essentially of a repeated invocation of the pscl model of computation under control of the real time counter t@ and the step counter s@ maintained by the environment:

At a given time interval t@, successive signal values in the carriers are computed by repetition of the pscl evaluation cycle until stabilization is obtained in all signal carriers declared in the description. The s@ counter is incremented with each required cycle and may control the termination of the evaluation after a predetermined number of steps in case of unstable situations (e.g. oscillations). Interpreter activity finstep is invoked automatically to provide default signal growth in all carriers on which no user activity is invoked in a given step.

After stabilization has been obtained the s@ counter is reset to 1 and the t@ counter incremented by 1. Interpreter activity finint is invoked on all carriers to determine the first signal value of the next real time interval.

The environment may now extend the signals held by the interface carriers of all description by one value, and may thus destabilize the state of the description again. Then the computation of step values is resumed as outlined above until again stabilization is obtained, and so forth.

5. Directions

To promote an orderly development of hardware description languages and to enhance their acceptance in an industrial environment, a construction mechanism for such languages, based on a common core syntax has been developed. This construction mechanism ensures that the semantics of the languages derived are well defined. Further, semantically related, languages can be constructed which permit the description of digital systems at different levels of abtraction. The common core syntax facilitates learning a new language written in the CONLAN framework. In addition, capabilities for syntax modification permit the suppression of unneeded constructs and the introduction of shorthand notation for frequently used objects to obtain simple yet useful languages.

Base CONLAN is primarily a starting point, with well-defined and semantically sound primitives, for language designers to derive a coherent and comprehensive family of digital system description languages. More time and effort will be needed before user oriented, less general but simpler, special purpose languages are developed. Timeliness in the distribution of this report is one reason for the absence of user level languages. But more importantly, the Working Group now seeks a broad spectrum of response from the community of users and language designers. It is expected that some user level languages will become at least de facto standards for purposes of communication throughout the computer establishment. It would be a mistake for the Working Group to publish languages which might be misinterpreted as proposed standards, but at the same time be regarded by the user community as, for some reason, inadequate.

With the publication of this report members of the Working Group and other toolmakers may regard Base CONLAN as fixed. The development of user level languages may now proceed without fear that they will become obsolete due to changes in the postulated base language.

A set of software tools to aid language construction based on CONLAN has been developed by R. Piloty and his associates at the University of Darmstadt[1] They include:

- a syntax development package,

- a syntax driven parser generator, and

- a name analysis and type checking package.

In addition a bcl simulator implementing an extended bcl - providing user operations on arrays of values, signals and carriers - is under development.

6. References

1. R. Piloty, M. Barbacci, D. Borrione, D. Dietmeyer, F. Hill, P. Skelly: "CONLAN - A Formal Construction Method for Hardware Description Languages: Basic Principles", Proceedings National Computer Conference, Volume 49, Anaheim, California, 1980.

2. R. Piloty, M. Barbacci, D. Borrione, D. Dietmeyer, F. Hill, P. Skelly: "CONLAN - A Formal

---

[1]Institut fuer Datentechnik, Technische Hochschule, D-6100 Darmstadt, F.R. Germany.

Construction Method for Hardware Description Languages: Language Derivation", Proceedings National Computer Conference, Volume 49, Anaheim, California, 1980.

3. R. Piloty, M. Barbacci, D. Borrione, D. Dietmeyer, F. Hill, P. Skelly: "CONLAN - A Formal Construction Method for Hardware Description Languages: Language Application", Proceedings National Computer Conference, Volume 49, Anaheim, California, 1980.

4. R. Piloty, M. Barbacci, D. Borrione, D. Dietmeyer, F. Hill, P. Skelly: "An Overview of CONLAN: A Formal Construction Method for Hardware Description Languages", Proc. IFIP Congress 1980, Tokyo Melbourne, October 1980.

5. R. Piloty, D. Borrione: "The CONLAN Project: Status and Future Plans", Proc. of the 19th ACM, IEEE Design Automation Conference, Las Vegas, Nevada, June 1982.

6. M.R. Barbacci: "A Comparison of Register Transfer Languages for Describing Computers and Digital Systems". IEEE Computer Society, Transactions on Computers, Volume C-24, Number 2, February 1975.

7. Special issue on Hardware Description Languages, IEEE Computer Society, Computer, Vol. 7, No. 12, Dec. 1974

8. Proceedings of the 2nd International Symposium on Computer Hardware Description Languages, Darmstadt, ACM German Chapter Lectures W - 1974.

9. Proceedings of the 3rd International Symposium on Computer Hardware Description Languages and their Applications, New York Sept. 3. - 5., 1975. IEEE Cat. No. 75 CH1010-8C

10. Proceedings of the 4th International Symposium on Computer Hardware Description Languages, Palo Alto, Oct. 8-9, 1979 IEEE Cat. No. 79 CH1436-5C

11. Special issue on Hardware Description Languages, IEEE Computer Society, Computer, Vol. 10, No. 6, June 1977

12. Collection of Proceedings of the IEEE, ACM Design Automation Conference.

13. Collection of Proceedings of the Fault Tolerant Computing Symposia.

14. R. Piloty: "Guidelines for a Computer Hardware Description Consensus Language" (2nd draft), Memorandum to the Conference on Digital Hardware Languages, June 6, 1976

15. P. Lucas, K. Walk: "On the Formal Description of PL/I", Annual Review of Automatic Programming, Vol. 6, part 3, 1969.

16. J. Mermet: "Etude methodologique de la Conception Assistee par Ordinateur des systemes logiques: CASSANDRE", These d'Etat, USMG, Grenoble, France, April 1973

17. B. Liskov, S. Zilles: "Programming with Abstract Data Types", SIGPLAN Notices 9, pp 50 - 59, April 1974

18. W.A. Wulf, R.L. London, M. Shaw: "Abstraction and Verification in ALPHARD", Technical Report, Department of Computer Science, Carnegie-Mellon University, March 1976

19. D. Borrione, J.F. Grabowiecki: "Informal Introduction to LASSO : a Language for Asynchronous Systems Specification and simulatiOn", Proc. EURO IFIP 79, London, September 1979

20. D. Borrione: "The Worker Model of Evaluation for Computer Description Languages", Proc. 5th Int'l Symposium on CHDL 81, North Holland Publ. Comp.

21. D. Borrione: "Langages de Description de Systemes Logiqùes : Propositions pour une methode formelle de definition", These d'Etat, USMG INPG, Grenoble, France, July 1981

22. C. Hewitt, H. Baker: "Actors and Continuous Functionals", IFIP Working Conference on Formal Description of Programming Concepts. St. Andrews, New Brunswick, Canada, August 1-5, 1977

23. C. Hewitt, H. Baker: "Laws for Communicating Parallel Processes", Proc. IFIP-77, Toronto, Canada, August 8-12, 1977

24. C. Hewitt: "Viewing Control Structures as Patterns of Passing Messages", Artificial Intelligence, Vol. 8 No. 3 (June 1977), pp 323 - 364

II CONLAN Concepts and Constructs

CONLAN is a family of languages for describing the behavior and structure of digital hardware, firmware, and software, and documenting the syntax and semantics of the family members. CONLAN "users" describe behavior and structure with existing family members. CONLAN "toolmakers" provide (i) new family members from existing members using CONLAN and (ii) software that supports the members of the family. CONLAN documents prepared by toolmakers specify syntax and semantics, but do not otherwise restrict supporting software. All members of the CONLAN family utilize the same basic syntax and semantics. Within limits toolmakers can extend or restrict syntax in working languages.

7. Basic Symbols

CONLAN is based upon the characters of the International Standard 7 Bit Coded Character Set for Information Processing Interchange (ISO 646) International Reference Version. In addition, an extended set of symbols may be used in CONLAN descriptions intended for publication only.

7.1. Characters and Symbols

Table 7-1 provides the ISO 646-IRV character set and codes (hexadecimal), and the CONLAN semantics of most characters. The character set is partitioned into (1) control characters, (2) capitals and letters, (3) digits, (4) space, and (5) symbols.

ISO 646-IRV codes 00 through 1F, and code 7F are treated as spaces by CONLAN implementations. The space (code 20, as well as codes 00-1F and 7F) may be used freely to enhance the readability of a CONLAN description. Spaces may not appear within compound symbols, keywords, or identifiers.

Elements of a list are separated by a comma (code 2C) or a semicolon (code 3B).

The semantics of symbols (?), (\), and (`) (codes 3F, 5C, and 60, respectively) may be assigned by CONLAN toolmakers.

Equipment may provide characters not listed in Table 7-1 in place of characters shown. An equipment dependent character may appear in CONLAN documents as a replacement for an ISO 646-IRV character with the same code. For example, the following substitution is made in this document:

$ for ¤

It is the responsibility of the toolmaker to provide the full ISO 646-IRV character set even when equipment to support an implementation does not. The international monetary symbol, (¤ , code 24) must be used to accomplish this.

Table 7-2 depicts the CONLAN predefined compound symbols and their semantics. Additional compound symbols can be defined by toolmakers via FORMAT@ statements (Section 11.4).

CONLAN documents destined for publication only may: (a) underline keywords or set them in bold face, and (b) replace implementation symbols as shown in Table 7-3.

Code	Character	Semantics	
00-1F		control characters (treated as space)	
20	space	terminator	
21	!	record access	
22	"	part of comment delimiter	
23	#	catenation	
24	¤	escape character	
25	%	delay	
26	&	logic AND	
27	'	string delimiter	
28	(	expression, tuple, and	
29	)	parameter list delimiters	
2A	*	multiply	
2B	+	positive, add	
2C	,	list separator	
2D	-	negative, subtract	
2E	.	compound identifiers, tuple denotation	
2F	/	divide, part of comment delimiter	
30-39	0 1 2 3 4 5 6 7 8 9		digit
3A	:	typing separator, subscript range, label	
3B	;	list separator	
3C	<	less than	
3D	=	equal	
3E	>	greater than	
3F	?	(available)	
40	@	used in system identifiers	
41-5A	A B C D E F G H I J K L M N O P Q R S T U V W X Y Z		capital
5B	[	subscript header	
5C	\	(available)	
5D	]	subscript terminator	
5E	↑	power	
5F	_	(underscore) used as letter in identifiers	
60	`	(available)	
61-7A	a b c d e f g h i j k l m n o p q r s t u v w x y z		letter
7B	{	enumerated set, time reference	
7C	|	logic OR	
7D	}	enumerated set, time reference	
7E	~	logic NOT	
7F	delete	treated as space	

Table 7-1: ISO 646-IRV Characters and CONLAN Semantics

SYMBOL	MEANING
>=	greater than or equal
=<	less than or equal
~ =	not equal
.<	set member
"/	comment head
/"	comment terminator
(.	tuple denotation head
.)	tuple denotation terminator
<|	derived from

Table 7-2: CONLAN Compound Symbols

V for |	logic OR
Λ for &	logic AND
¬ for ~	logic NOT
≥ for >=	greater than or equal
≤ for =<	less than or equal
≠ for ~ =	not equal
∈ for .<	set member

Table 7-3: Publication Symbols

7.2. Keywords, Identifiers, and Comments

Keywords are sequences of capitals (Table 7-1) possibly terminated by symbol @. The character immediately following a keyword must be a space or a symbol. Keywords ending with symbol @ may be used in language definitions only, i.e., within CONLAN segments (Section 10.7) only. All sequences of capitals, letters, digits, underscore (_), and symbol @ that begin with "END" are interpreted as keyword END. Recommended statement termination keywords are suggested in the pertinent sections. The sequences of capitals and symbol @ listed in Table 7-4 are keywords of all members of the CONLAN family.

ACTIVITY	ALL	ASSERT	ATT	BODY	CARRY
CARRYALL	CASE	CLASS	CONLAN	DECLARE	DEFERRED@
DESCRIPTION	ELIF	ELSE	END	EXTEND	EXTERNAL
FORALL@	FORMAT@	FORONE@	FORSOME@	FUNCTION	FROM
IF	IMPORT	INTERPRETER@	IN	INOUT	IS
MEANS	OUT	OVER	PRIVATE	REFLAN	REPEAT
RETURN	REMOVE	STATIC	STEP	SUBTYPE	THE@
THEN·	TO	TYPE	USE	W	WITH

Table 7-4: CONLAN Family Keywords

CONLAN entities, such as types, elements of types, languages, descriptions, operations are generally named using identifiers starting with at least one letter followed by an arbitrary string of letters, digits, and symbol underscore (_) (Table 7-1), of any length and terminating with a letter or digit (user identifiers) or with the symbol @ (system identifiers). The character immediately following an identifier must be a space or a symbol. Identifiers ending with symbol @ may be used in language definitions only, i.e., within CONLAN segments (Section 10.7) only.

Certain primitive operations are provided with an infix format in which the operation is referenced through a symbol or a symbol string instead of an identifier (e.g., +). Toolmakers may provide, via FORMAT@ statements (Section 11.4) prefix and infix symbol strings or identifiers to denote new operations.

Commentary information can be included in a CONLAN document by enclosing an arbitrary string (the comment) inside ("/) and (/"). The "end of comment" (/") can not appear in the comment string.

8. CONLAN entities

CONLAN is concerned with the following entities:

1. Objects

2. Operations

3. Types

4. Classes

5. Descriptions and Instances of Descriptions

6. Languages

To denote an entity, either a standard denotation, or a construct for naming and defining this entity is provided.

A constant denotation is associated, in pscl, with all primitive objects which are not or do not contain cells. An infix operator symbol is associated with the most common primitive functions, in addition to a standard prefix notation. Other members of the CONLAN family will provide additional constant denotations and operator symbols for their primitive value objects and operations, respectively. In the general case, an identifier is associated with an entity at the point of definition/declaration.

The name of an entity is obtained by prefixing its identifier with the name of the enclosing entity if there is one. If no ambiguity arises, an entity name can be abbreviated by eliminating the redundant prefix of the name chain.

8.1. Objects

Objects serve as operands for operations. Pscl provides

- as simple value objects integers, booleans and strings.

- lists of objects ("tuples") as the basic structured objects

• simple carrier objects, called "cells".

A carrier may contain another object and is provided with suitable operations to change its content. Bcl provides more elaborate structured objects derived from tuples: carriers, signals, records and arrays. Other members of the CONLAN family are expected to provide flipflops, registers, memories as more complex container objects. Objects are collected into sets which may or may not be explicitly named.

For all value objects of pscl as well as for tuples constructed from value objects, a standard denotation is provided by the syntax of pscl. For cells no standard denotation exists. A cell is brought into existence and is named by a DECLARE statement (Section 11.3).

The DECLARE statement may be used also to associate an identifier with an object for which a standard denotation exists or for which another name has been declared previously (renaming).

8.2. Operations

In CONLAN two types of operations are known:

• functions   • activities

A function specifies a formal rule for the selection of a result object from a designated set of objects, while an activity specifies a formal rule for the modification of at least one carrier object. The effect of evaluating an operation is usually dependent on one or more supplied operands. The formal rule refers in this case to operand parameters, i.e., a list of identifiers, each representing a possible operand taken from a designated domain of entities.

The evaluation of the formal rule is normally specified in terms of already known operations. FUNCTION and ACTIVITY segments (Section 10.1) are provided as language constructs for this purpose. Operations whose formal rule is implied are called "primitive". Typical primitive functions of pscl are "plus" or "minus" or "equal" on integers, "and" and "or" for booleans. There is only one primitive activity in pscl, namely "put@", which replaces the content of a cell.

In CONLAN, generic operations are available to avoid repetitive writing of similar definitions. A generic operation has one or more attribute parameters to be bound to

• a type from a class (Section 8.3)

• an operation from a specific set of operations.

In the latter case, this set is denoted by an operation designator (Section 8.3.3) of the following form:

FUNCTION (list of type−designators): type−designator
ACTIVITY (list of type−designators)

Thus the operation designator specifies

• the kind of operation (i.e. function or activity)

• the number, type and access right of its operands

- the expected result type (functions only).

As an example

ACTIVITY x(f: FUNCTION(bool,bool): bool)

specifies that a formal function parameter f may be bound only to a binary boolean function returning a boolean value.

FUNCTION y(act: ACTIVITY(W bvar(0),bvar(0))): sometype

specifies that a formal activity parameter act may be bound to an actual two parameter activity with access right "writeable" (keyword W) for its first parameter and access right "readonly" (no keyword) for its second parameter.

Operations are invoked by stating their name together with the list of actual parameters in prefix notation. Operator symbols, for example for infix notation, may be introduced by syntax modification via FORMAT@ statements as an alternative (Section 11.4).

Invocation may be unconditional or conditional using conventional IF and CASE statements (Section 11.1.9).

8.3. Types and Classes

8.3.1. Object Types

An object type, or simply "type", is a named set of objects together with operations defined on the members (elements) of that set. The set of objects is called the domain of the type. TYPE and SUBTYPE segments are provided as language constructs for defining the domain and operations of a new type in terms of the domain and operations of an existing parent type and for associating an identifier as the name of this new type. This process is called "type derivation". Thereby the domain of the new type is always defined as a subset of the domain of its parent type. Every type in CONLAN is derived from some other type except one root type, the universal type "univ@". Its domain comprises all objects of CONLAN.

Families of object types may be derived with one or more formal attribute parameters. Such definitions provide a "family" of object types, e.g., a family of flipflop types with time attribute parameters for propagation delay, with an implied class of all family members.

A type retaining all operations of the parent type i.e., having only a restricted domain, may be defined as a subtype. It is taken equivalent to the parent type with respect to type checking (Section 8.3.3).

A type is named by compounding the identifier of the type definition segment with the names of all the enclosing segments. If no ambiguities arise, the type name can be abbreviated by eliminating the redundant prefix of the name chain. For instance, the full name of type 'int' is 'pscl.int'. Assuming a type 'dff' defined in a segment 'seq' of a description 'control',its full name would be 'control.seq.dff'; however it might be unambiguous to refer to it as 'seq.dff', or even 'dff', depending on the circumstances.

8.3.2. Generic Types - Classes

A type family is called "generic" if at least one of its formal parameters is itself to be bound to a type, from a given set of types called a class. The class of each of these generic parameters must be specified using the designator of this class (Section 8.3.3).

A class can be defined in two ways:

1. explicitly, with a CLASS definition segment (Section 10.6), which is provided as a language construct for defining a set of types and for associating an identifier as a name for this new class. The domain of this new class is defined in terms of the domain of an existing parent class. As with types the domain of the new class is a subset of the domain of its parent class. This implies that there is a root class, the universal class any@, having no parent class. Its domain comprises all object types in CONLAN, defined or yet to be defined.

2. implicitly, with the definition of a type family in a TYPE segment (Section 10.3), which not only provides a family of object types, but also the class, whose domain consists of all family members. This class is implicitly assigned the name of the type family prefixed by "class_". Its domain is formed as a subset of the domain of any@, which therefore is its parent class.

All classes have the operations '=', '~=', '<|', '.<' and 'designate@' in common. It is important to note that the elements of a class are _types_, not the elements of these types.

As an example, a CLASS value_type may be explicitly defined having the types "int", "bool" and "string" as its domain. With this class a generic type family

$$\text{TYPE value\_cell(t: value\_type)}$$

may be defined with three members, namely "value_cell(int)", "value_cell(bool)" and "value_cell(string)", which are the domain of the implicitly defined CLASS class_value_cell.

As an aid for the toolmaker to specify the type checking and parameter matching rules for a particular CONLAN member (Section 8.3.3) three reserved class names are provided to name the most important classes of types involved in these rules:

CLASS **val_type** to define all value types of a given member language (empty in pscl). Values, the elements of value_types, are static objects, i.e., they do not change over time. Values possess a standard denotation.

CLASS **sig_type** to define all signal types of a given member language (empty in pscl). Signals, the elements of signal types, are sequences of values over time.

CLASS **carr_type** to define all carrier types of a given member language. Carriers are objects which may contain other objects and whose content may be modified (written) by suitable operations. They possess no standard denotation and, consequently, must be named via DECLARE statements.

In pscl the existence of classes **any@** and **carr_type** is implied (Section 14). In derived languages the three basic classes val_type, sig_type and carr_type must be explicitly defined using the class definition segment.

8.3.3. Strong Typing - Type Checking

Experience with programming languages has revealed the value of requiring users of a language to specify the set of which each referenced entity is a member, i.e., to specify the type of all identifiers used. While hardware description languages have not provided traditional data types (integer, real, complex, etc.), many have introduced hardware types (register, terminal, clock, switch, etc.). To gain error checking capability CONLAN requires that for every identifier representing an object, operation or instance of a description a designator is specified at the point where this identifier is introduced.

This designator identifies a set or family of entities which are related by some common property, such as a common type definition for objects, a common domain and range for operations or a common description for an instance of a hardware unit. Designators are found in formal parameter lists, predicate forms, set constructors, instantiation of descriptions, and declarations.

There are four categories of designators:

1. type designators

> type_name
> type_name(actual_attributes)
> type_designator_expression

a type_designator_expression is a compile time expression that yields a type_designator.

2. class designators

> class_name
> class_name(actual_parameters)

3. operation designators

> ACTIVITY
> ACTIVITY(type_designators)
> FUNCTION : type_designator
> FUNCTION(type_designators) : type_designator

4. description designator

> description_name
> description_name(actual_attributes)

The set to which an entity belongs is denoted using the following formats:

$$\text{entity\_identifier: designator}$$

As usual constants are an exception to strong typing. Standard denotations are provided for them. Therefore they do not need to be declared and designated explicitly. To enhance readability no effort has been made to keep the constant denotations for the elements of different types disjoint. For example, 0 and 1 are standard constant denotations for booleans and integers as well. Furthermore, constant denotations for the elements of a derived object type are automatically inherited from its parent type.

Consequently the type of a constant denotation is determined during type checking by ascertaining that this denotation is legitimate in the domain of the formal type in the operand position where the denotation occurs. If this check is successful, the formal type is taken as actual, otherwise an typing error is noted.

Type checking of designated parameters is done by comparing designators of formal and actual parameters. Normally formal and actual type designators must be identical. Exceptions are the following:

1. Non-matching actual types may be converted explicitly to the required formal type and vice versa using special operations "old(x)", "new(x)", "convert@(x,t)" in object type segments (Section 10.5).

2. Subtype designators are taken as compatible with the designators of their parent types.

3. Automatic invocation of parameter matching operations at compile time may be introduced for a given language by explicitly defining suitable INTERPRETER@ operations (Section 10.1.8) along with the other operations of their object types e.g., a FUNCTION sig(x) for automatic dereferencing a carrier to the signal which it contains. Invocation of these parameter matching operation is governed by a parameter matching table. It specifies the matching operation to be invoked for each possible combination of type classes val_type, sig_type and carr_type to which the type of a formal and actual parameter may belong (for bcl see Section 17.3.3). For pscl there is no automatic invocation of parameter matching operations.

8.4. Descriptions and Instances of Descriptions

Hardware units or modules may be described in CONLAN using DESCRIPTION segments as a language construct (Section 10.2). A DESCRIPTION segment associates an identifier with an interface carrier list, and a body describing either the functional relation between the contents of the interface carriers or the structural decomposition into submodules, or mixed forms from both.

DESCRIPTION segments may be parameterized by one or more formal attribute parameters, to avoid repetitive specification. Such definitions provide a family of descriptions. A member of the family is obtained by binding all formal attribute parameters with actual attributes.

The functional relation is usually specified by a list of activity invocations (conditional and unconditional) referring to the interface carriers and declared local carriers as needed (behaviour description).

Structural decomposition is expressed in terms of nested instances of descriptions, which specify the sub-units used. The language construct to name an instance of a given description (Section 8.3.3) is the USE statement (Section 11.3). For example the statement

USE m1, m2, m3: amod ENDUSE

associates three identifiers m1, m2, m3 to three instances of description amod. An instance of a description communicates with its environment through a set of interface carriers. The number, names, types and direction of communication (IN, OUT, INOUT) of its interface carriers are specified in the defining description segment (Section 10.2).

Interface carriers are brought along with each instance (implied carrier declaration) by the USE statement. Thereafter, each interface carrier may be referenced by prefixing its identifier with the instance name. For example, if description amod has four interface cells x1,..., x4, 'm3.x1' refers to the first interface cell of instance m3 of amod.

8.5. Languages

A new member of the Conlan language family is specified by

- its reference language

- a collection of object types, free standing operations, classes and descriptions (module types) as its semantic entities

- a (possibly empty) set of format statements to modify the reference language syntax.

A language definition segment (Section 10.7) is provided to derive a new member la2 of the CONLAN family of languages from an existing member la1. Its format is

REFLAN la1 CONLAN la2 BODY.....ENDla2

In the body, a toolmaker may write any number of TYPE, CLASS, ACTIVITY, FUNCTION and DESCRIPTION segments to define the semantic entities of the new language la2 in terms of those of the reference language la1. FORMAT@ statements (Section 11.4) may be used to modify the syntax of the reference language, either to delete productions which are no longer needed for the user, or to add productions to provide notations for new syntactic entities.

Semantic entities defined in the segment for the new language la2 may be referenced in all segments stating la2 as their reference language. In particular, they may be used to define a further language, if la2 is referenced in the REFLAN part of the corresponding CONLAN segment.

As outlined in Section 2.4, two ways are available to the toolmaker to restrict the accessability of semantic entities involved in the derivation of la2 from la1:

1. Entities defined by segments in la2 can be made inaccessible to segments using la2 as a reference language by prefixing these segments with keyword PRIVATE.

2. Segment names in la2 terminated with symbol "@" are only accessible in CONLAN segments with la2 as a reference language (i.e., for language definition).

In addition, to avoid redefinition, entities from the old language la1 may be brought forward to the new language la2 using CARRY and CARRYALL statements.

9. Block Structure

A CONLAN text consists of properly nested blocks. Blocks which define an entity such as a type, a language, a hardware module or an operation, are called "segments". Blocks which refer to or invoke an instance of a segment such as declarations, operation invocations, etc. are called "statements". Segments begin with a keyword followed by an identifier and terminate with keyword END, which may, but need not be followed by the segment identifier. Most statements begin with a keyword and terminate with END or ENDxxx where xxx reflects the opening keyword. There is one exception to this rule: "Operation Invocation" (Section 11.1) is not bracketed by keywords.

9.1. Segments and Statements

The segments, the sections in which they are presented, and their principal intended application are:

FUNCTION   Define operations that return an element of a type or class (Section 10.1). The keyword FUNCTION, when used as a designator (Section 8.3.3), stands for the set of all functions.

ACTIVITY   Define operations that do not return an element of a type and thus can not be used in expressions. The keyword ACTIVITY, when used as a designator (Section 8.3.3), stands for the set of all activities.

DESCRIPTION   Define types of hardware modules (Section 10.2).

TYPE   Define new object types (Section 10.3 and 8.3.3).

SUBTYPE   Denote a subset of a type or a member of a family (Section 10.4).

CLASS   Define sets of types (Section 10.6).

CONLAN   Define new working languages (Section 10.7).

The statements, the sections in which they are presented, and their principal intended application are:

FORALL@   Test if a predicate is true for all members of a set (Section 11.1.2).

FORSOME@   Test if a predicate is true for at least one member of a set (Section 11.1.3).

FORONE@   Test if a predicate is true for exactly one member of a set (Section 11.1.4).

THE@   Select the member of a set for which a predicate is true (Section 11.1.6).

"Set enumeration"
              Denote an unordered set of objects (Section 11.1.5).

ALL   Select all members of a set for which a predicate is true (Section 11.1.7).

"Direct invocation"
:   Function and Activity invocation (Section 11.1.8).

IF
:   Evaluate one of several operations depending on several predicates (Section 11.1.9).

CASE
:   Evaluate one of several operations depending on the value of a conditional or selection expression (Section 11.1.9).

OVER
:   Specify textual repetition of activity invocations over members of a set (Section 11.1.10).

RETURN
:   Evaluate the result of a function invocation (Section 11.1.11).

REFLAN
:   Define the reference language for a segment (Section 11.2).

DECLARE
:   Declare an element of a type (Section 11.3).

USE
:   Name an instance of a description (Section 11.3).

FORMAT@
:   Define a syntax modification (Section 11.4).

CARRY
:   Bring selected segments defined in another segment (Section 11.5).

CARRYALL
:   Bring all segments defined in another segment (Section 11.5).

ASSERT
:   Predicates that result in error reports if they evaluate to false (Section 11.6).

IMPORT
:   Make objects of an enclosing segment accessible (Section 11.7).

9.2. Reference Languages

The outermost segment of a CONLAN text requires a "reference language". That reference language specifies the existing language to be used as a base for the definition of the new segment (languages themselves are defined via CONLAN segments, Section 10.7). A reference language brings via their names functions, activities, types, classes and descriptions to inner segments. Such global names provide a starting point for forming the body of segments.

9.3. Naming Rules

Names are used in CONLAN to reference objects and segments. They can be simple names (identifiers) or compound names. A compound name is a simple name prefixed with the (simple or compound) name of the segment which directly encloses the declaration/definition point of the simple name. Thus a compound name can be a chain of simple names starting with the outermost segment name and reflecting the segment nesting structure. The parts of a compound name are separated by periods.

9.3.1. General Rule

Each object or segment of a CONLAN text must be uniquely referable by its compound name. This implies that the same simple name must not be introduced twice in the same segment. In most cases however, with regard to the restrictions mentioned in Section 9.3.3 and 9.3.4, it will be sufficient to denote an entity by its simple name.

There are no forward references for names in CONLAN. No name is known and can be used before it has been defined.

9.3.2. Scope of Names

Names can be introduced at various points in a CONLAN text. They are introduced always in the form of a simple name (identifier). The scope of a name is the region of text in which the entity designated by such a name is known i.e., potentially referable. An entity is referable in a segment other than the segment where it is introduced only according to the importing rules (Section 10) of that segment. If an entity is exported in accordance with the exporting rules of the enclosing segment, the scope of the name of this entity is extended to the end of the scope of that segment name.

1. The scope of the name of a FUNCTION, ACTIVITY, DESCRIPTION, TYPE, SUBTYPE, CLASS or CONLAN segment extends from its introduction in the header of the segment to the end of the directly enclosing segment. If there is no enclosing segment, the scope of the name of the outer segment only covers that segment.

2. Additionally, a CONLAN segment name may be referenced by REFLAN statements of other segments.

3. The scope of a formal parameter name of a FUNCTION, ACTIVITY, TYPE, SUBTYPE, CLASS or DESCRIPTION segment extends from its introduction to the end of the segment.

4. The scope of names introduced by a DECLARE or USE statement extends from its declaration to the end of the directly enclosing segment.

5. An IMPORT statement does not introduce a new name. It only affects the importing rules.

6. The scope of names introduced in a CARRY list extends from that CARRY list to the end of the directly enclosing segment.

7. The scope of a name introduced by an ALL, FORALL@, FORSOME@, FORONE@ or THE@ statement is just the following predicate. Such a name can be referenced only as a simple name.

8. The scope of a name introduced by an OVER statement is only the following activity_invocation_list. Such a name can be referenced only as a simple name.

9.3.3. Rules for Referencing Entities

If an entity is introduced in the manner of cases 1, 3, 4, 6, 7 or 8 of Section 9.3.2, it may have the same simple name as an entity defined or declared in an enclosing segment. In that case, the entity introduced in the segment may be referenced by its simple name, whereas the entity of the enclosing segment can be referenced only be its compound name. This implies that an entity imported by an IMPORT statement must be referenced by its compound name when another entity with the same simple name is introduced in the importing segment.

9.3.4. Overloading of Operation Names

FUNCTION or ACTIVITY segments defined in (or named in CARRY lists of) different segments may have the same simple name without hiding one another, if the type of at least one formal parameter or of the result is unique. They may be referenced by their simple name or infix operator, if the operation to be invoked can be determined unambiguously from the actual context. Such an operation name is said to be overloaded.

If the operation cannot be determined unambiguously from the actual context (e.g., because of ambiguous constant denotations or parameter matching rules), then the operation must be referenced by its compound name. Note: A function name cannot overload an activity name and vice versa.

9.3.5. Implicit Compound Names

Operations listed in the CARRY list of a TYPE segment must be defined within the TYPE segment of the defining type. If operations to be carried are only denoted by simple names, they are implicitly prefixed with the name of the defining type.

10. Segments

The different language segments are introduced by displaying a template which illustrates the main syntactic features, keywords, optional and required components, etc. The templates are no substitute for the formal syntax and are given here only to improve the clarity of the explanations.

When presenting the templates for the different segments, a '*' in the templates indicates those parts that may appear in any order that does not reference a yet to be defined entity.

10.1. FUNCTION and ACTIVITY Segments

Operations are abstractions used to model the behavior of hardware, firmware and software. Operations are first defined with the appropriate segment, and then invoked in the operation_invocation parts of other segments.

10.1.1. Operation Templates

An operation that performs some computation and returns a member of a type is defined according to the template in Figure 10-1. If the set of optional components following keyword BODY is empty the keyword BODY can be omitted.

An operation that performs some computation but does not return a member of a type, is defined

reference_language	(optional, Section 11.2)
FUNCTION	(required)
identifier	(required, Section 7.2)
(parameters)	(optional, Section 10.1.2)
: type_designator	(required, Section 8.3.3)
assertions	(optional, Section 11.6)
BODY	(optional, see below)
assertions	*(optional, Section 11.6)
type_definitions	*(optional, Section 10.3)
subtype_definitions	*(optional, Section 10.4)
class_definitions	*(optional, Section 10.6)
operation_definitions	*(optional, this section)
element_declarations	*(optional, Section 11.3)
import_statements	*(optional, Section 11.7)
operation_invocations	(optional, Section 11.1)
assertions	(optional, Section 11.6)
RETURN result_expression	(required, Section 11.1.11)
format_statements	(optional, Section 11.4)
ENDidentifier	(required)

Figure 10-1: Function Segment Template

according to the template in Figure 10-2.

Assertions are predicates on the parameters and local objects that are expected to be true. These predicates are evaluated when the operation is under evaluation (Section 19.3). If an assertion evaluates to false, an error condition exists.

The result_expression of a FUNCTION segment computes the object returned by the function.

The parameters of operations are divided into three categories:

- Modifiable or Writeable (Keyword W)

- Input (no Keword)

- Attribute (Keyword ATT)

Only the second and third category of parameters (inputs and attributes) are applicable to functions.

W   The types of the parameters in this category must be of CLASS carr_type. These
           parameters may be referenced by operation invocations inside the body of the operation

reference_language	(optional, Section 11.2)
ACTIVITY	(required)
identifier	(required, Section 7.2)
(parameters)	(optional, Section 10.1.2)
assertions	(optional, Section 11.6)
BODY	(required)
assertions	*(optional, Section 11.6)
type_definitions	*(optional, Section 10.3)
subtype_definitions	*(optional, Section 10.4)
class_definitions	*(optional, Section 10.6)
operation_definitions	*(optional, this section)
element_declarations	*(optional, Section 11.3)
import_statements	*(optional, Section 11.7)
operation_invocations	(required, Section 11.1)
assertions	(optional, Section 11.6)
format_statements	(optional, Section 11.4)
ENDidentifier	(required)

Figure 10-2: Activity Segment Template

          segment in W positions (i.e., be written) as well as in input positions (i.e., be read). W parameters may also be written or read in the environment in which the activity is invoked.

Input   Parameters in this category may be of any type. They may be referenced in input positions (i.e., be read) by the operation invocations inside the body of the operation segment. In the environment, in which this segment is used, input parameters may be read and, if they are of CLASS carr_type, written.

ATT   Parameters in this category are used to specify elements of any object type or operation type or class that select a segment out of a family of similar segments. ATT parameters are bound at compile time and are neither read nor written during execution.

10.1.2. Parameter Lists for Operation Definitions

Formal parameter lists for function and activity segments are enclosed in parentheses unless the lists are empty in which case the parentheses are also omitted.

A sublist of input parameters of a particular type consists of the parameter names separated by commas and followed by a colon and the type designator (Section 8.3.3). Sublists of modifiable parameters must be preceded with the keyword W. Sublists of attribute parameters must be preceded with the keyword ATT.

Parameter lists in activity definition segments consist of sublists of input, W, and ATT parameters separated by semicolons. Parameter lists in function definition segments consist of sublists of input and ATT parameters only. There may be any number of these sublists in a parameter list. For example:

act(a,b:type1;W c,d:type2;e,f:type3;W g,h:type4;ATT i,j:type5;ATT k,l:type6)

a,b,e,f are input parameters; c,d,g,h are Writable parameters; i,j,k,l are ATTribute parameters.

An operation segment is generic if the designator of at least one of its formal parameters is a class designator (Section 8.3.2) or an operation designator (Section 8.3.3).

Any number and combination of such parameters is permissible, provided that generic and non-generic parameters are ordered so as to avoid forward references. Nested definitions and uses of generic operations are allowed. Generic parameters can only appear as ATT parameters.

Generic operations may be defined by toolmakers only. They provide a family of operations and thereby simplify the toolmaker's task.

10.1.3. Parameter Lists for Operation Invocation

No keywords, type designators, or semicolons are included in the actual parameter lists for function or activity invocations. The actual parameter lists will consist of a list of actual parameters separated by commas. A formal parameter in the definition list will be bound to the actual parameter in the invocation list occupying the corresponding position in the invocation parameter list. Obviously, the number of formal and actual parameters must be identical.

The types of the actual and formal parameters are compared according to the principles for type checking outlined in Section 8.3.3 to determine error conditions and the possible need for parameter matching operations as specified in the parameter matching table of the reference language.

In pscl no parameter matching operations are invoked at compile time. Consequently no parameter matching table exists. The parameter matching table for bcl is found in Section 17.3.3.

For generic parameters, the actual parameter must be a segment of the class specified by the formal parameter:

formal	actual
any@	type designator
class_identifier	type designator
class_identifier(actual_parameters)	type designator
ACTIVITY	activity name
ACTIVITY(formal_parameters)	activity name
FUNCTION:type_designator	function name
FUNCTION(formal_parameters):type_designator	function name

Actual attribute parameters corresponding to generic formal attribute parameters designated with any@ or 'class identifier' (i.e., 'type' parameters) must have the operations used in the body of the generic segment. Actual attribute parameters corresponding to generic formals designated with FUNCTION or ACTIVITY (i.e., 'operation' parameters) must be used in accordance to the normal type checking rules.

10.1.4. Nesting Rules for FUNCTION and ACTIVITY Segments

FUNCTION and ACTIVITY segments may appear under item "operation_definitions" of the CONLAN, DESCRIPTION, FUNCTION, ACTIVITY and TYPE segment templates. However, STATIC operations (10.1.7) can not appear in the operation_definitions of a non-STATIC operation.

10.1.5. Importing Rules for FUNCTION and ACTIVITY Segments

1. FUNCTION and ACTIVITY segments know and have access to all FUNCTION, ACTIVITY, TYPE, SUBTYPE and CLASS segments defined in the reference language, Section 11.2.

2. FUNCTION and ACTIVITY segments know and have access to all FUNCTION, ACTIVITY, TYPE, SUBTYPE and CLASS segments defined in all enclosing segments.

3. FUNCTION and ACTIVITY segments have access to the external objects and segments represented by the formal parameters of those segments.

4. FUNCTION and ACTIVITY segments have access to the external objects mentioned in an IMPORT statement. An IMPORT statement is valid only, if the next enclosing segment is a FUNCTION, ACTIVITY, or DESCRIPTION segment. An IMPORT statement may contain only objects which are accessible to the next enclosing segment.

5. FUNCTION and ACTIVITY segments have access to objects and segments represented by formal attribute parameters of enclosing segments.

10.1.6. Exporting Rules for FUNCTION and ACTIVITY Segments

No names declared or defined inside a function or activity, including the formal parameters, are available outside the segment.

10.1.7. STATIC Operations

Unless otherwise specified, FUNCTION and ACTIVITY segments can be invoked recursively. The contents of carriers declared inside one of these segments are not retained across successive invocations. All of these properties can be reversed by prefixing the operation definition segment with the keyword STATIC:

    STATIC FUNCTION name(parameters): type_designator ... ENDname
    STATIC ACTIVITY name(parameters) ... ENDname

STATIC operations can not be invoked recursively, carriers declared inside one of these segments retain their contents across operation invocations. STATIC operations can not be invoked from or nested in non-STATIC operations. However, non-STATIC operations can be invoked from and nested in STATIC operations. Both STATIC and non-STATIC operations can be invoked from or nested in the bodies of DESCRIPTION segments.

10.1.8. INTERPRETER@ Operations

Selected operation definitions may be prefixed with keyword INTERPRETER@ to indicate that the operation can be invoked by the interpreting environment. Typically these operations supply default carrier modification mechanisms (Section 17.3) or parameter matching operations (Section 17.3.3).

> INTERPRETER@ FUNCTION name(parameters): type_designator ... ENDname
> INTERPRETER@ ACTIVITY name(parameters) ... ENDname

10.1.9. EXTERNAL Operations

Operation segments contained in some external file of existing segments may be made visible within a given operation segment with:

> EXTERNAL FUNCTION name_list ENDEXTERNAL
> EXTERNAL ACTIVITY name_list ENDEXTERNAL

Such segments can be viewed as an addition to the reference language of the given operation segment. This implies that the external segments must be written in the same reference language. The mechanism for accessing the external source is implementation dependent.

10.2. DESCRIPTION Segments

Descriptions are used to define hardware module types together with their interface carriers. When a description is defined, all instances of the description are created and placed in an unnamed set. Instances are named via USE statements (Section 11.3).

10.2.1. Description Template

New descriptions are introduced according to the template shown in Figure 10-3. The attributes of a description are used to define a family of descriptions. They are bound to compile time expressions at the point of instantiation.

The interface_list of a description specifies the hardware interface of the unit described. All communication is via this interface. Interface parameters are divided into three categories, depending on the direction of information flow.

IN
Interface parameters in this category may be of any object type. IN parameters may be read but not written in the body of the segment. IN parameters may be read or written in the environment in which the segment is used.

OUT
The types of interface parameters in this category must be object types of CLASS **carr_type**. OUT parameters may be read or written in the body of the segment. OUT parameters may be read but not written in the environment in which the segment is used.

INOUT
The types of interface parameters in this category must be object types of CLASS **carr_type**. INOUT parameters may be read or written by both the body of the segment and the environment in which the segment is used.

reference_language	(optional, Section 11.2)
DESCRIPTION	(required)
identifier	(required, Section 7.2)
(attributes)	(optional)
(interface_list)	(optional)
assertions	(optional, Section 11.6)
BODY	(required)
assertions	*(optional, Section 11.6)
type_definitions	*(optional, Section 10.3)
subtype_definitions	*(optional, Section 10.4)
class_definitions	*(optional, Section 10.6)
operation_definitions	*(optional, Section 10.1)
description_definitions	*(optional, Section 10.2)
object_declarations	*(optional, Section 11.3)
description_instantiations	*(optional, Section 11.3)
operation_invocations	(optional, Section 11.1)
assertions	(optional, Section 11.6)
ENDidentifier	(required)

Figure 10-3: Description Segment Template

10.2.2. Parameter Lists for Description Definitions

Formal interface and attribute parameters of descriptions are enclosed in separate lists.

A sublist of parameters of a particular type consists of the parameter names separated by commas and followed by a colon and the type designator (8.3.3). Sublists of interface parameters of the same type must be preceded with one of the keywords specifying the direction of information flow (IN, INOUT, or OUT).

Formal interface and attribute parameter lists consist of sublists of parameters of the same type separated by semicolons. There may be any number of these sublists in a parameter list.

10.2.3. Nesting Rules for DESCRIPTION Segments

DESCRIPTION segments may appear under item "description_definitions" of the CONLAN (Section 10.7.1) and the DESCRIPTION (Section 10.2.1) segment template.

10.2.4. Importing Rules for DESCRIPTION Segments

1. DESCRIPTION segments know and have access to all segments defined in the reference language, Section 11.2.

2. DESCRIPTION segments know and have access to all segments defined in all enclosing segments. However, this does not permit recursive use of DESCRIPTIONs.

3. DESCRIPTION segments do not have access to objects declared in enclosing segments. All communications with their environment is done through their interface parameters.

4. DESCRIPTION segments have access to objects named in the formal parameter list of directly enclosed descriptions by compounding the formal parameter with the name of an instance of that internal description. (This includes descriptions brought in as EXTERNAL segments, Section 10.2.6.)

5. DESCRIPTION segments have access to objects represented by formal attribute parameters of enclosing segments.

10.2.5. Exporting Rules for DESCRIPTION Segments

DESCRIPTION segments make available to enclosing segments only the parameters named in the interface list. In an enclosing segment the formal interface parameter names must be compounded with the name of an instance of the description. Attributes can not be referenced in an enclosing segment.

10.2.6. EXTERNAL Descriptions and Operations

Description and operation segments contained in some external file of existing segments may be made visible within a given description segment with:

EXTERNAL DESCRIPTION name_list ENDEXTERNAL
EXTERNAL FUNCTION name_list ENDEXTERNAL
EXTERNAL ACTIVITY name_list ENDEXTERNAL

Such segments can be viewed as an addition to the reference language of the given description segment. This implies that the external segments must be written in the same reference language. The mechanism for accessing the external source is implementation dependent.

10.3. TYPE Segments

When a type is defined, class any@ is augmented with the type. Its elements are specified as a subset of a parent type and thus ultimately as a subset of univ@. Elements of carrier types (CLASS carr_type) are named via DECLARE statements (Section 11.3). Elements of non-carrier types inherit their constant denotation from the parent type.

10.3.1. Type Template

New types are introduced according to the template in Figure 10-4. All parameters to a TYPE segment are attributes. The keyword ATT preceding the parameter list is not necessary. As indicated in Section 8.3.2 a parameterized TYPE segment introduces not only a family of object types but also the class of all family members.

TYPE	(required)
identifier	(required, Section 7.2)
(parameters)	(optional)
BODY	(required)
set_definition	(required, see below)
carry_list	(optional, Section 11.5)
type_definitions	*(optional, Section 10.3)
subtype_definitions	*(optional, Section 10.4)
class_definitions	*(optional, Section 10.6)
operation_definitions	*(optional, Section 10.1)
format_statements	*(optional, Section 11.4)
ENDidentifier	(required)

Figure 10-4: Type Segment Template

The set_definition provides the set of elements of the type in terms of an already defined parent type (Section 8.3.3), by enumeration (Section 11.1.5), or by construction (Section 11.1.7).

The carry_list lists all non-private operations defined in the prior type which are needed in the new type.

10.3.2. Nesting Rules for TYPE Segments
TYPE segments may appear under item "type_definitions" of FUNCTION, ACTIVITY, TYPE, CONLAN and DESCRIPTION segment templates.

10.3.3. Importing Rules for TYPE Segments

1. TYPE segments know and have access to FUNCTION, ACTIVITY, TYPE, SUBTYPE and CLASS segments defined in the reference language (Section 11.2).

2. TYPE segments know and have access to FUNCTION, ACTIVITY, TYPE, SUBTYPE and CLASS segments defined in all enclosing segments.

3. TYPE segments have access to objects and segments represented by formal attribute parameters of enclosing segments.

10.3.4. Exporting Rules for TYPE segments

1. TYPE segments make available to the outside world those FUNCTION and ACTIVITY segments, which are defined directly within them and which are not prefixed with keyword

PRIVATE. No internal TYPE, SUBTYPE or CLASS segments are available to enclosing segments.

2. TYPE segments also make available those FUNCTION and ACTIVITY segments of the defining type, which are explicitly carried with a CARRY statement (Section 11.5).

10.4. SUBTYPE Segments

SUBTYPE	(required)
identifier	(required, Section 7.2)
(parameters)	(optional)
BODY	(required)
set_constructor	(required, Section 11.1.7)
ENDidentifier	(required)

Figure 10-5:   Subtype Segment Template

SUBTYPE segments (Figure 10-5) may be used to derive a new type from an existing type, or a member of a parameterized type family, when all operations of the existing type are desired for the new type. No new operations may be introduced. Parameters and results are as defined in the parent type. Operations are performed in the parent type. If the context requires the result of an operation to be in the subset, but it in fact lies outside the subset, an error condition exists. This is part of the normal type checking mechanism outlined in Section 8.3.3.

SUBTYPE segments may appear anywhere a TYPE segment can appear and are subject to the same nesting, import, and export rules.

Example:
    SUBTYPE positive_integer BODY
        ALL a: int WITH a > 0 ENDALL
    ENDpositive_integer

10.5. Type Relations and Type Conversions
The domain of a type or subtype may be specified in several ways:

1. as a true subset of the domain of an existing type or subtype t1 using a subset constructor, e.g.,:

$$ALL\ x:t1\ WITH\ pred(x,a,b)\ ENDALL$$

2. identical to the domain of an existing type or subtype t1 by simply writing its designator, e.g.,:

t1

3. by enumeration of constant denotations (TYPE segments only), e.g.:

$$\{0,1,'U'\}$$

In cases (1) and (2) t1 is called the defining or parent type.

In case (3) the defining type is the universal type univ@.

Type and subtype designators, may be used as operands in type relations:

1. Two types or subtypes s, t are equal (s=t) if s and t refer to the same TYPE or SUBTYPE definition segment.

2. Let s and t designate two types or subtypes. Then t is derived from s (t $<|$ s) if and only if s is equal to t, or t is a subtype of s, or s is the defining type of t, or the defining type of t is derived from s. Thus, type derivation is a transitive relation.

3. Let x represent an element of univ@ and t the designator of any type or subtype in CONLAN. Then x is an element of t (x $.<$ t) if it is an element in the domain of t.

Within the body of a TYPE segment that is derived from a prior type or subtype, representatives of the new objects are a priori of the new type. In addition, constant denotations in the defining type are inherited by the elements of the new type or subtype.

In order to enforce type compatibility when defining operations of a new type in terms of operations of the defining type, three type conversion functions are provided:

1. When invoking an operation of the defining type, objects of the new type or subtype can be used as parameters by explicitly converting them to the defining type via:

$$old(expression)$$

2. When invoking a function of the defining type, results of the defining type can be explicitly converted to the new type, if the returned element is also in the domain of the new type, via:

$$new(expression)$$

3. Parameters, which are not of the new or defining type may be converted to specific destination types via:

$$convert@(expression,destination\_type\_designator)$$

if the result of the expression is also in the domain of the specified type. The result of convert@ is an element of the specified destination type. Application of convert@ is only permitted if the type of the result returned by the expression is derived from the destination type or vice versa.

Conversions of type by old, new and convert@ are not allowed outside of TYPE segments. Convert@ may only be used by toolmakers in language definition segments.

10.6. CLASS Segments

A CLASS segment is used to define a subset of the universal class any@, and to associate with it an identifier as a class name. The class name may be used later to designate formal type parameters, i.e., to restrict the range of types to which a formal parameter of a generic segment may be bound, and to define parameter matching tables (e.g., for bcl in Section 17.3.3) and types admissible in W positions of activities.

10.6.1. CLASS Template

CLASS   (required)
identifier   (required)
(parameters)   (optional)
BODY   (required)
set-definition   (required, see below)
ENDidentifier   (required)

Figure 10-6: Class Segment Template

New classes are introduced according to the template in Figure 10-6. CLASS segments are used to denote a subset of an existing parent class. Similary to SUBTYPE segments all operations are carried from the existing class. Hence, all operations from the universal class any@ are available in all derived classes. Operations are performed in class any@.

The set definition provides the set of the types which form the domain of the new class in terms of an already existing class by enumeration (Section 11.1.5) or by construction (Section 11.1.7). In the case of enumeration the universal class any@ is taken as the parent class.

Example:

    CLASS value_types
     BODY
     ALL x: any@ WITH x<| bool | x <| int | x <| string ENDALL
    ENDvalue_types

A CLASS segment may appear anywhere a TYPE segment is allowed and is subject to the same nesting, import, and export rules.

As indicated in Section 8.3.2 classes can also be implicitly defined. For example, the CLASS class_value_cell, implicitly defined with the introduction of the type family value_cell(t: value_types), corresponds to the pseudo definition[2]:

---

[2]FORONE@ predicate does not apply to a parameter t representing a type, member of a class

```
CLASS class_value_cell BODY
ALL x: any@ WITH
    FORONE@ t: value_type IS x = value_cell(t) ENDFORONE
ENDALL
ENDclass_value_cell
```

10.7. CONLAN Segments

10.7.1. CONLAN Template

reference_language	(required, Section 11.2)
CONLAN	(required)
identifier	(required, Section 7.2)
BODY	(required)
carry_list	(optional, Section 11.5)
type_definitions	*(optional, Section 10.3)
subtype_definitions	*(optional, Section 10.4)
class_definitions	*(optional, Section 10.6)
operation_definitions	*(optional, Section 10.1)
description_definitions	*(optional, Section 10.2)
format_statements	*(optional, Section 11.4)
ENDidentifier	(required)

Figure 10-7: Language Definition Segment Template

A new member of the CONLAN family of languages may be defined according to the template in Figure 10-7. The carry_list enumerates the segments to be brought to the new language from the reference language.

10.7.2. Nesting Rules for CONLAN Segments
CONLAN segments may not be nested in other segments.

10.7.3. Importing Rules for CONLAN Segments
CONLAN segments know and have access to all nonPRIVATE segments defined in their reference language (Section 11.2).

10.7.4. Exporting Rules for CONLAN Segments

To all segments stating a given CONLAN segment as their reference language via a REFLAN statement (Section 11.2) the following segments are available:

1. all nonPRIVATE segments defined directly inside this CONLAN segment.

2. all segments of the reference language of this CONLAN segment which are explicitly carried by a CARRY statement (Section 11.5) inside the CONLAN segment.

11. Statements

11.1. Operation Invocation Statements

In FUNCTION, ACTIVITY, and DESCRIPTION segments, the operations listed in the operation_invocations part are executed concurrently. Function invocations may be nested and non STATIC functions may, in addition be recursive. The order of evaluation is affected by operator precedence, the use of parentheses, and the statement used to invoke the operation.

An expression is a string of object denotations, identifiers, constructors, function denotations (either infix or prefix), '(', and ')'. An object_expression denotes a rule for selecting an object of a type. A set_expression denotes a rule for selecting one or more elements of a set. Depending on the context, the term "expression" will stand for either a object_expression or a set_expression.

11.1.1. Predicate Expressions

A predicate is any expression that produces a boolean result. We symbolize such expressions with "pred(a,b,...)", where the parameters are sets or objects that appear in the symbolized expression.

Examples:
$4 < 5,$
$a = 10,$
$5 + 1 = 9,$
$4 < 5 \& (a = 10)$

11.1.2. FORALL@ Predicate

FORALL@ x: type_designator IS pred(x, a, b, ...) ENDFOR

This predicate evaluates to true if the embedded predicate is true for all elements of the designated type (Sec 8.3.3). If the type is empty, FORALL@ evaluates to true.

Example: FORALL@ i: int IS i >= 0 ENDFOR   produces 0

11.1.3. FORSOME@ Predicate

FORSOME@ x: type_designator IS pred(x, a, b, ...) ENDFOR

   This predicate evaluates to true if the embedded predicate is true for at least one element of the designated type (Section 8.3.3). If the type is empty, FORSOME@ evaluates to false.

11.1.4. FORONE@ Predicate

FORONE@ x: type_designator IS pred(x, a, b, ...) ENDFOR

   This predicate evaluates to true if the embedded predicate is true for exactly one element of the designated type (Section 8.3.3). If the type is empty, FORONE@ evaluates to false.

11.1.5. Set Enumeration
   An unordered set of objects is denoted via a list of object denotations enclosed in set delimiters { and } and separated by commas. Listed elements are of type univ@. The list may be empty.

Example: {0, 1, 'X', 'a', abc}

11.1.6. Element Selection

THE@ x: type_designator WITH pred(x, a, b, ...) ENDTHE

   This operation selects the member of the designated type for which pred(x, a, b, ...) evaluates to true. If the predicate is true for more than one element or no elements of the designated type an error condition exists.

11.1.7. Subset Construction

ALL x: type_or_class_designator WITH pred(x, a, b, ...) ENDALL

   This operation selects the set of all elements of the designated type or class for which pred(...) is true. The empty set is selected if there are no elements of the designated type or class, for which pred(...) is true.

11.1.8. Direct Invocation
   In direct operation invocations, a function or activity name may be listed together with actual parameters, separated by commas, and enclosed in parentheses. (The parentheses must be given even if no parameters are required.) If an infix invocation notation was prescribed via a format statement, that notation may be used.

Examples:
    act(5),   "/prefix operation invocation/"
    f(3)+4,   "/expression/"
    a:=b+c   "/infix invocation of the assign activity/"

Sub-expressions are invoked in the order given by the operator precedence (Section 13.7). NonSTATIC operators can be invoked recursively.

11.1.9. Conditional Invocation

With pred, pred1, ... being predicates and fa, fa1, etc. being function or activity invocations:

IF pred THEN fa ELSE fb ENDIF

evaluates fa if pred = 1, and evaluates fb otherwise.

IF pred1 THEN fa1 ELIF pred2 THEN fa2 ELSE fa3 ENDIF

evaluates fa1 if pred1 = 1, otherwise evaluates fa2 if ~pred1&pred2 = 1, otherwise evaluates fa3 if ~pred1&~pred2 = 1.

Any number of ELIF clauses may be present. Their order affects in general the result of the evaluation: the fa of the first predicate (from the left) that is true is evaluated. All fa must be operation invocations of the same type (i.e., all function invocations or all activity invocations). In a conditional activity invocation the ELSE clause is optional. In a conditional function invocation the ELSE clause is mandatory.

One of many potential invocations may be chosen with:

CASE x IS
x1: fa1;
x2: fa2;
...
ELSE fa   (optional)
ENDCASE

x denotes an expression returning a value. All xi must denote different values. All fai must be operation invocations of the same type (i.e., all function invocations or all activity invocations). Fai is evaluated if expression x evaluates to value xi. If the ELSE clause is present and if x evaluates to none of the listed xi, then fa is evaluated. The ELSE clause is mandatory when invoking functions if not all possible values of x are covered. It is optional when invoking activities.

11.1.10. Repeated Invocation

Multiple concurrent invocations of the same operation may be expressed by:

OVER x FROM i STEP j TO k REPEAT fa(parameters) ENDOVER
OVER y: set REPEAT fa(parameters) ENDOVER

where x, i, j, k are integers and set is finite; x and y may be used as actual parameters. The "STEP j" clause is optional. If it is not present, j defaults to 1 (if i=<k) or -1 (if i>k).

11.1.11. Result Expression

RETURN expression

The result expression in a FUNCTION segment is evaluated once, after all other operation invocations are terminated. The value is then returned to the invoking expression.

11.2. REFLAN Statements

The existing CONLAN language in which a segment is written is revealed with:

REFLAN language_identifier

The language_identifier is a CONLAN segment identifier. All nonPRIVATE segments defined in the named CONLAN segment are made available for use in the segment prefixed with the REFLAN statement.

11.3. DECLARE and USE Statements

Elements of types and instances of descriptions are created when the TYPE or DESCRIPTION segment is defined. However, except for those types which provide a constant denotation for their elements (e.g., int, bool, tuple@, etc.), elements of types can not be referenced in a segment unless an identifier is explicitly provided for each one of them through a DECLARE statement. Likewise, since no standard denotation exists for instances of a description, those instances of descriptions which are to be used in a segment must be provided with an identifier through a USE statement.

11.3.1. DECLARE Statement

Elements of types may be named via DECLARE statements of the form:

DECLARE identifier : type_designator ENDDECLARE

If several elements of the same type are being declared, the list of their identifiers may be grouped before specifying the ':type_designator'. In a DECLARE statement which does not rename a previously referenceable element (see below), each declared identifier names a different element.

Example: DECLARE a, b: ivar(0); c: btml(0) ENDDECLARE

In this example, a and b are elements of type ivar(0) and c is an element of type btml(0). For types that provide a constant denotation for their elements, a specific element may be named with:

DECLARE identifier: type_designator = constant_denotation ENDDECLARE   or
DECLARE identifier: type_designator = expression ENDDECLARE

In the latter case, the expression must be a compile time expression. For types that do not provide a constant denotation for their elements, one or more specific elements, or parts thereof, if already declared can given synonymous names with:

DECLARE identifier : type_designator = expression ENDDECLARE

The expression may only invoke selection and catenation operators, and all operands must be previously declared identifiers. The expression is evaluated at compile time and must return an element of the designated type.

Examples for introduction of synonyms:

DECLARE

  max1: int = 10;   "/for a constant denotation/"

  max2: int = max1 + 5;   "/for a value returned by a compile time expression/"

  ibit: brtv(0);

  opflag: brtv(0) = ibit   "/opflag synonymous to ibit/"

ENDDECLARE

11.3.2. USE statement

Instances of descriptions, representing the structural decomposition of a system into subsystems or modules are named via USE statements. They are not invoked, initiated or terminated. They function continuously from the moment when they are named. USE statements may be written in two forms for specifying module intercommunication.

Form 1: Intercommunication via explicit activity invocations

    USE identifier dimensions: description_designator(attributes) ENDUSE

Form 2: Intercommunication via common interface carriers

    USE identifier(actual_interface_parameter_list): description_designator(attributes) ENDUSE

Actual interface parameters are matched by position to formal parameters. If one or more actuals are missing in the use statement, the corresponding empty places must be displayed by consecutive commas.

Dimensions and attributes are optional. If in form 1 dimensions are stated (e.g., m[1:10;1:5]) then a corresponding number of instances of the same module type are specified, which may be later referenced by appending an index to the instance identifier (e.g., m[2,5]). Note: Indexing of multiple instances at the point of reference (e.g., m[1,]) is not allowed.

If several instances of the same description with the same actual attributes are being used, the list of their identifiers may be grouped before specifying the ':description_designator'. Each identifier names a different instance. Example:

    USE m1[1:4],m2,m3[1:5]: module(5,7) ENDUSE

The USE statement not only provides a name for an instance of a description but also implicitly declares all its interface carriers. Any interface carrier can be referenced in the segment where the instance is being used by compounding the instance name with the formal interface carrier name, e.g. m1.x2 where m1 is the instance name and x2 the formal carrier name.

If form 2 is used the following rules in specifying actual parameters must be observed:

1. In an interface position which requires a carrier, the name of an actual carrier may be inserted and thus be declared synonymous with the interface carrier name which corresponds to this position. Alternativly it may be left empty. The name of an actual carrier in an interface parameter position may be the name of an either implicitly or explicitly declared carrier.

2. An interface parameter position which does not require a carrier must always be bound to an actual parameter expression returning an object of the type corresponding to this position.

3. An interface carrier of a description instance is considered as implicitly declared after the specification of the description designator of this instance. It may only be referenced behind this specification, i.e. forward references of interface carrier names are not permitted.

The following example illustrates both forms of module instanciation:

Assume: DESCRIPTION amod(i: pint)(IN x1, x2: btm0; OUT y: btm0; INOUT z: bbus)
        BODY........
        ENDamod

        DECLARE a, b: btm0; c: bbus ENDDECLARE

where btm0 and bbus designate boolean terminals and busses, respectively for which unidirectional (symbol '.=') and bidirection (symbol '.=.') connection activities are assumed to be defined

        USE m1, m2: amod(3) ENDUSE   (form 1)
implicitly provides

        DECLARE m1.x1, m1.x2, m1.y, m2.x1, m2.x2, m2.y: btm0; m1.z. m2.z: bbus ENDDECLARE

This permits the explicit specification of intercommunication with unidirectional and bidirectional connections.

        m1.x1 .= a, m1.x2 .= m2.y, m2.x1 .= b, m2.x2 .= m1.y, m1.z .=. m2.z

The corresponding network is shown in Figure 11-1.a.

Another version of this network may be specified by

        USE m1(a,,,c): amod(3); m2(b, m1.y, m1.x2,c): amod(3) ENDUSE   (form 2)
This form implicitly declares

        DECLARE m1.x1: btm0 = a;
            m1.x2, m1.y: btm0;
            m1.z: bbus = c;
            m2.x1: btm0 = b;
            m2.x2: btm0 = m1.y,
            m2.y: btm0 = m1.x2;
            m2.z: bbus = c ENDDECLARE

This shows that form 2 establishes intercommunication by declaring carriers synonymous with implicitly declared internal and predeclared external carriers. An empty carrier position in an actual parameter list of a description instance indicates the declaration of a new carrier. In contrast a filled parameter position introduces a synonymous name for an already declared carrier. The corresponding version of the network is shown in Figure 11-1.b.

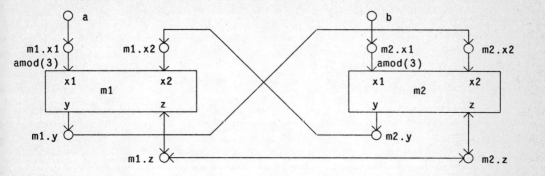

(a) Explicit Interconnections

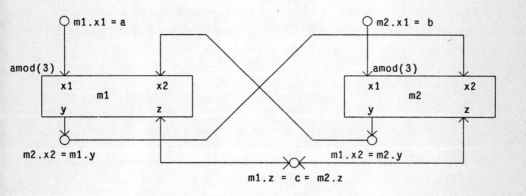

(b) Common Interface Carriers

Figure 11-1: Module Intercommunication

11.4. FORMAT@ Statements

In CONLAN syntax extensions may be specified with:

DEFERRED@	(optional)
FORMAT@	(required)
REMOVE remove_part	*(optional)
EXTEND extend_part	*(optional)
ENDFORMAT	(required)

The remove_part consists of a list of production and/or alternative identifiers. This list specifies the productions or alternatives to be removed. Removing a production implies removal of all its alternatives. It is the toolmaker's responsibility to remove all uses of the production from the rest of the grammar.

The extend_part is used to specify new productions or new alternatives of an existing poduction. A production is identified by the name of the non-terminal (i.e., the left hand side of the BNF rule). The pointer to an alternative is the pointer to the production followed by '.', followed by an integer index associated with the alternative. These integers do not need to be consecutive but must be unique within the set of alternatives for a production.

New productions can be protected by specifying a list of modification rights:

R(emove)   This production can be removed in a future CONLAN segment but the name of the non_terminal can not be used for a new production (i.e., it can be deleted but not replaced).

E(xtend)   Alternatives can be added to this production.

Alternatives can be marked with

R(emove)   This alternative can be removed in a future CONLAN segment. If a production is marked by R only the complete production may be removed, not single alternatives. If a production is not marked with R but every alternative is marked with R each alternative can be deleted, but at least one alternative must remain. The restrictions are only valid for future CONLAN segments, but not for the currently written segment. If there are no modification rights this production is neither extensible nor removable.

The syntax for the new alternative or production must be specified using the same meta-notation described in Part V.

The semantics specification follows the MEANS keyword and is to be written using the constructors, predicates, etc. available in the language. To avoid confusion, the MEANS clause must not make use or take advantage of the extension currently being defined.

The MEANS clause is optional. For instance, when several productions are being added, only the root(s) might have a need for semantic specifications, although of course this can not and should not be a limitation. When the MEANS clause is given without a bnf_extension, the semantic specifications are added to those already present in the production or alternative indicated by the index.

The keyword "DEFERRED@" is used to specify the visibility of the FORMAT@ statement. Omitting the keyword "DEFERRED@" means all extensions and removals of this FORMAT@ statement become visible (i.e. take effect) after processing the ENDFORMAT. Using DEFERRED@ the FORMAT@ statement will be visible after the END of the language segment.

To allow the MEANS part to refer to the productions, alternatives, etc. of the syntactic specification part, the non_terminals can be referenced with special symbols (argument_tag):

1. If the non_terminal to be referenced is part of the current alternative, i.e., the alternative to which the MEANS part belongs, then this reference is denoted by "@" followed by the index of the non_terminal in this alternative.

2. If the non_terminal is part of another predefined syntactic alternative, the index must be prefixed by '@', followed by the identifier of that alternative.

For instance, let's assume we want to extend the language to allow the use of "[" and "]" in accessing an array. Assume that an element of a multidimensional array a is selected by a function extract(a,s) where s is a LISP-like tuple of indices so far denoted by (.i,(.j,(.k,.....).).). To introduce a new denotation a[i j k ....] for the array selection the following FORMAT@ statement has to be written, where maketuple(x,y) yields (.5,7.) for $x=5$ and $y=7$:

FORMAT@
EXTEND array_access.6   "/a new alternative for array_access/"
  R = identifier '[' i_list ']'
  MEANS extract(@1,@2)
EXTEND i_list.3   "/a new alternative for i_list/"
  E = integer i_list
  MEANS maketuple(@i_list.3.1,@i_list.3.2)   "/a fully qualified
                                            reference to non_terminals/"
ENDFORMAT

Notice that the new alternative for "array_access" can be used in any future languages but can not be modified or replaced. At most, a future language designer can eliminate it. The production for "i_list" can be extended in future languages by adding alternatives. Presumably, these will be newer formats for specifying the indices of an array.

11.5. CARRY Statements

Segments defined in an existing language and made available to the writer of a new language segment via a reference language statement (Section 11.2), are not available to the user of the new language segment, unless explicitly carried with:

  CARRY segment_list ENDCARRY   or
  CARRYALL

In carrying a parameterized segment to a new language segment, care must be taken that all types required by the formal parameter list or as a result type must be carried also to this language to permit referencing, invocation or instantiation of the parametrized segment by the user of the language.

When a new type is defined as a subset of an existing type, or as a member of an existing (parameterized type) family, the existing type must be used in the set definition part of the new type. Selected or all operations defined on this existing type may be brought to the new type with:

    CARRY operation_list ENDCARRY   or
    CARRYALL

Parameters and results of carried operations which were of the old type are automatically converted to the new type. The types of all other parameters and results are not changed. That is, within the new type, carried operations from the previous type are readily available. Section 10.5 describes mechanisms for explicit type conversion available to the toolmakers.

If an operation listed in the CARRY statement has an infix notation (it may be a primitive symbol, or a symbol introduced via a syntax extension) the new meaning is automatically added to the semantics of that symbol.

For example, assume the following TYPE definition:
```
TYPE t1
    BODY
    FUNCTION f(x, y: t1): bool .... ENDf
    FUNCTION g(x: t1; y: int): t1
        RETURN .....
        FORMAT@
        EXTEND exp6.10
            R = exp6 'XL' exp7                          "/syntax/"
            MEANS g(@1,@2)                              "/semantics/"
        ENDFORMAT
    ENDg
ENDt1
```

Then, the definition:
```
TYPE t2
    BODY
    ALL u: t1 WITH ..... ENDALL
    CARRY f, g ENDCARRY                         "/extend the meaning of f and g/"
    .....
ENDt2
```

is equivalent to:

```
TYPE t2
    BODY
    ALL u: t1 WITH ..... ENDALL
    FUNCTION f(x, y: t2): bool                    "/explicit definition of f/"
        RETURN t1.f(old(x), old(y))                     "/type conversion/"
    ENDf
    FUNCTION g(x: t2; y: int): t2                 "/explicit definition of g/"
        RETURN new(t1.g(old(x), y))                     "/type conversion/"
        FORMAT@
        EXTEND exp6.10
            MEANS t2.g(@1,@2)                         "/extend semantics/"
        ENDFORMAT
    ENDg
    .....
ENDt2
```

In the FORMAT@ statement of t2.g, above, alternative 10 of production exp6 is given an additional meaning, without redefining or extending the production. @1 and @2 refer to the nonterminals defined in the FORMAT@ statement given in t1.g (the creation of alternative 10 of production exp6).

11.6. ASSERT Statements

Conditions on actual parameters, global objects, results, attributes, etc. that ensure appropriate invocation or instantiation of segments are expressed in assertion statements of the form:

   ASSERT predicate_list ENDASSERT

Assertions can appear in several places in an operation segment definition. Assertions appearing after the parameter list and before the body, can only refer to objects provided in the formal parameter list or via the importing rules. These assertions are evaluated before the operations invocation part is evaluated. Assertions appearing after BODY and before the operations invocation part can only refer to objects declared in the operation definition segment, objects provided in the formal parameter list, or objects provided via the importing rules. These assertions are evaluated before the operations invocation part. Assertions appearing after the operations invocation part can refer to the same objects mentioned in the previous class, but are evaluated after the operations invocation part has terminated and before the return expression (in the case of a FUNCTION segment) is evaluated.

For DESCRIPTION segments all assertions must be true at every interval of time after an instantiation. See Chapter 19.3 for complete details on the evaluation algorithms.

11.7. IMPORT Statements

The IMPORT statement is a device to avoid repetitive writing of actual parameter lists if an operation is to be invoked repeatedly with the same actual parameters (e.g., data registers to be read and/or written by a micro operation). It may be used within a FUNCTION or an ACTIVITY segment to import objects, accessible in the immediate enclosing FUNCTION, ACTIVITY or DESCRIPTION segment without passing them through the parameter list of this operation.

Example: IMPORT a, b; W c, d; e

Keyword <u>W</u> in the object list affects the access right of the following sublist, i.e., a, b and e may be read only, c and d read and written in the current segment. An object which is not writeable in the enclosing segment may not be imported with a W access right. Only in ACTIVITY segments may objects be imported with W access rights.

It should be noted that the IMPORT statement does <u>not</u> introduce new objects; it only affects the visibility of existing objects.

In the evaluation model directly imported objects will be treated as additional actual parameters.

III Primitive Set CONLAN

12. Introduction
Primitive Set Conlan (pscl) is the root language from which all other members of the CONLAN family are derived. As a consequence

1. it has no reference language,

2. the domains of its object types are assumed rather than defined,

3. the operations of its object types are assumed rather than defined in terms of more primitive operations.

In particular it serves as the reference language for the formal definition of Base Conlan, which comprises the Conlan concepts for hardware description in space and time. Its primitive object types and classes are chosen to be simple and yet provide a very general base for construction of higher operative languages (Section 13 and 14).

An evaluation algorithm for pscl is provided (Section 15) to the toolmaker to specify unambiguously how invoked operations from the pscl object types and instanciated descriptions are to be evaluated by his/her implementation.

13. Pscl Object Types and Operations
In pscl there are three broad categories of objects: "Scalar Values" are static objects; they do not change with time. Type "int", "bool" and "string" are the basic pscl types whose domains are scalar values. "Scalar Carriers" are named objects which may contain other objects and whose content may be changed over time by suitable activities. Type "cell@" is provided by pscl as a primitive scalar carrier type from which others may be derived. "Ordered Sets" are objects consisting of an indexed sequence of other objects. Type "tuple@" in pscl provides a general domain of ordered sets from which other types of this category can be derived.

Table 13-1 depicts the types and operations which exist in pscl. The table shows, for each type, the domain and range of its operations. These types and operations are described in more detail subsequently.

13.1. int
Type int consists of all integers, together with a substantial number of functions provided without formal definition, i.e., they are "known." An integer is denoted with a contiguous sequence of symbols, digits and capitals that may be partitioned into the sign part, magnitude part and base indicator. The sign part consists of symbol "+" (optional) or symbol "-". The magnitude may be expressed in decimal, binary, octal, or hexadecimal using the digits (and capitals) appropriate to the base indicator as shown in Table 13-2.

Example: $-12 = -1100B = -14O = -CH$

TYPE	OPERATION	INFIX OPERATOR	DOMAIN	RANGE	FUN/ACT
int	equal	=	int x int	bool	F
	notequal	~=	int x int	bool	F
	less	<	int x int	bool	F
	lessequal	=<	int x int	bool	F
	greater	>	int x int	bool	F
	greaterequal	>=	int x int	bool	F
	plus	+	int x int	int	F
	minus	-	int x int	int	F
	times	*	int x int	int	F
	divide	/	int x int	int	F
	power	↑	int x int	int	F
	mod	MOD	int x int	int	F
bool	equal	=	bool x bool	bool	F
	notequal	~=	bool x bool	bool	F
	less	<	bool x bool	bool	F
	lessequal	=<	bool x bool	bool	F
	greater	>	bool x bool	bool	F
	greaterequal	>=	bool x bool	bool	F
	and	&	bool x bool	bool	F
	or	|	bool x bool	bool	F
	not	~	bool	bool	F
string	equal	=	string x string	bool	F
	notequal	~=	string x string	bool	F
	less	<	string x string	bool	F
	lessequal	=<	string x string	bool	F
	greater	>	string x string	bool	F
	greaterequal	>=	string x string	bool	F
	order@		string	int	F
cell@(t: any@)	get@		cell@	t	F
	put@		cell@ x t		A
	empty@		cell@	bool	F
tuple@	equal	=	tuple@ x tuple@	bool	F
	notequal	~=	tuple@ x tuple@	bool	F
	size@		tuple@	int	F
	select@		tuple@ x int	univ@	F
	extend@		tuple@ x univ@	tuple@	F
	remove@		tuple@ x int	tuple@	F
univ@	equal	=	univ@ x univ@	bool	F
	notequal	~=	univ@ x univ@	bool	F

Table 13-1: Pscl Types and Operations

NUMBER SYSTEM	BASE INDICATOR	DIGITS AND CAPITALS AVAILABLE TO EXPRESS MAGNITUDE
decimal	none	0 1 2 3 4 5 6 7 8 9
binary	B	0 1
octal	O	0 1 2 3 4 5 6 7
hexadecimal	H	0 1 2 3 4 5 6 7 8 9 A B C D E F

Table 13-2: Integer Denotation

13.2. bool

Type **bool** has two members, denoted by 1 and 0 representing "true" and "false" respectively, together with operations '=', '~=', '&', '|', '~', '<', '=<', '>', '>='. The relational operators are based upon '0' being less than '1'.

13.3. string

Type **string** consists of all sequences of characters, together with operations '=', '~=', '<', '=<', '>', '>=', and order@. The objects of string are denoted by enclosing the sequence in single quotes ('). Sequences such as '1A', 'b + 5', are included. The character ' must be doubled if it is to appear in a string denotation (e.g., 'What''s his name?').

The relational operators are based on the order of characters in the ISO-646 table. When comparing strings of different length, the shorter string is extended with trailing spaces (code 20) to equalize the lengths.

Function order@ takes a string as parameter and returns an integer computed by treating the elements of the strings (i.e., the characters) as 'digits' in a base 128 representation. The leading character is the most significant 'digit'. For instance, order@('Xy2') returns $(58H*128*128 + 79H*128 + 32H)$, that is, 163CB2H.

13.4. cell@

Generic type family **cell@(t: any@)** defines the primitive carrier types known in pscl. Each member type comprises an infinite number of simple carrier objects each of which may hold at most one element of type t at any point in time. This element is called its content.

No standard denotation exists for cells. A cell must be named in a declaration statement before it can be referenced in an operation. Cells are initially empty.

Function empty@(x) returns 1 ('true') if cell x is empty otherwise it returns 0 ('false').

Function get@(x) returns the contents of cell x. If the cell x is empty an error condition exists.

Activity put@(x,u) replaces the content of cell x with u. The type of u must be the specified content type of cell x. An attempt to put an element of the wrong type result in an error. If cell x is empty, put@ simply inserts u in the cell.

Cells are potentially modifiable objects (via activity put@). These are the only pscl objects with this property and constitute the basis for the development of carriers, variables, and other modifiable objects in the CONLAN family.

13.5. tuple@

Type tuple@ consists of all lists of elements of univ@ (Section 13.6) together with operations '=', '~=', size@, select@, remove@, and extend@. Tuple@ includes the empty list.

A tuple is denoted via a list of object denotations enclosed in '(.' and '.)', and separated by commas.

Two tuples are equal ('=') if they have the same size and identical members in identical order. Otherwise they are not equal ('~=').

Function size@(x) returns the number of members of a tuple. If the tuple is empty, size@ returns 0. Consecutive integers from 1 to size@(x) identify the positions of the members of tuple x. Only the positions of this range may be referenced. Attempts to reference positions outside this range result in an error report.

Function select@(x,i) returns the member of tuple x in position i (if integer i is in the range 1 through size@(x)).

Function remove@(x,i) returns the tuple y such that y holds all components of x in the same order except the ith one if i is in the range from 1 to size@(x). If i is outside the range, an error condition. If size@(x) = 1 then the empty tuple is returned.

Function extend@(x,u) returns the tuple y of size@(x)+1 such that the components of y are identical to those of x in its leftmost size@(x) positions and that the component in position size@(x)+1 is equal to u.

13.6. univ@

Type univ@ consists of

1. all elements of all types defined or yet to be defined in CONLAN and DESCRIPTION segments.

2. the fully specified designators of these types.

Type univ@, however, does not contain itself as an element. It permits the present definition of operations involving objects to be defined in the future. Only the operators '=' and '~=' are defined in univ@. The pscl universe consists of all integers, booleans, strings, cells and tuples and their type designators. This universe, enumerated in part, is:

$$univ@ = \{..,-1,0,+1,..,'!',..,0,(.0,0.),...,'xYz',..pscl.int,pscl.bool,...\}$$

Type univ@ is considered as the defining type for the other types of pscl, namely "int", "bool", "string", "cell@", "tuple@" from which all other types of CONLAN will be derived.

13.7. Operator Precedence

In an expression that invokes symbolized (infix) operators, where parentheses do not dictate the order of invocation, operators are invoked in order of decreasing precedence numbers. There are nine levels of operator precedence in CONLAN, as shown in Table 13-3.

Precedence	Operators	
1	|	(disjunction)
2		to be assigned in bcl
3	&	(conjunction)
4	= ~= < =< > >= .< <|	(relationals, member, derived)
5	+ -	(binary arithmetic)
6	* / MOD	(binary arithmetic)
7	↑	(power)
8	~ - +	(negation, unary arithmetic)
9		to be asigned in bcl

Table 13-3: Operator Precedence

Operators with the same precedence are invoked in the left to right order of their appearance. Operators may be added or removed via FORMAT@ statements (Section 11.4). The precedence of the symbols given in the table is fixed throughout CONLAN: An operator can be removed, but if reinserted, it must have the same precedence number.

14. Pscl Classes

Table 14-1 shows the operations on members of all classes.

OPERATION	INFIX OPERATOR	DOMAIN	RANGE
equal	=	any@ x any@	bool
notequal	~ =	any@ x any@	bool
type_derived	<|	any@ x any@	bool
class_derived	<|	any@ x P(any@)[3]	bool
element	.<	univ@ x any@	bool
member	.<	any@ x P(any@)	bool
designate@		univ@	any@

Table 14-1: Class Operations

---

[3]P(any@) = powerset of any@

14.1. any@

Class any@ is the universal class in CONLAN. Its domain is the set of all types defined or yet to be defined in all members of the CONLAN family, together with operations '=', '~=', '<|', '.<' and 'designate@'. The types forming the domain of a class are denoted by their designators. At this point in the development of CONLAN:

$$any@ = \{pscl.univ@, pscl.int, pscl.bool, pscl.tuple@, pscl.string,$$
$$pscl.cell@(pscl.int), pscl.cell@(bool),...\}$$

Function type_derived ('<|') may be used to determine if a member of any@ (a type) was derived from another member of any@.

Function class_derived ('<|') may be used to determine if a member of any@ (a type) was derived from another member of a specified class.

Function element ('.<') may be used to determine if an element of univ@ is also in the domain of a specified type.

Function member ('.<') may be used to determine if a type is a member of a specified class.

Function designate@ is used (e.g in definition of records in Section 18.11) to convert a type designator from univ@ to a member of any@ which can stand in a designator position.

Operations '=', '~=', '<|' ,'.<' and 'designate@' are automatically carried to any class derived from any@ using the CLASS definition segment (Section 10.6). They are performed in any@.

14.2. carr_type

CLASS carr_type designates all carrier types in pscl which may be defined in segments with pscl as a reference language in addition to members of carrier type family cell@, which are provided by pscl itself. It is defined as all types derived from some type cell@(t) and used to check the types permitted in W positions of the formal parameter lists of activities and in the OUT and INOUT positions of the formal interface list of descriptions defined in segments with pscl as their reference language.

15. Pscl Model of Computation

15.1. Basic Concepts of the Evaluation Model

This chapter introduces a semantic model, which has been specifically elaborated for CHDL's, called the Worker Model of Evaluation [20,21]. This model has been inspired by the Actor Model of Hewitt [22,23,24]. Then, the semantics of the various categories of segments, and of the primitive objects, operations and statements of pscl are defined in terms of this model. This implies that the rules for the evaluation of any pscl text are specified using the Worker Model.

Just as the text of a CONLAN segment does not dictate how software is to realize the operations defined in that segment, the presentation of the CONLAN evaluation algorithm in this part of the report does not dictate implementation details. It only present specifications that must be met by software or a human reader of CONLAN text. For example, a simulator running on a sequential processor must provide the effect of concurrency via sequential calculations.

The evaluation of a CONLAN text may be compared to a task to be performed in a mill. A number of workers are present; in fact there are as many as needed. There is one boss who is responsible for starting the evaluation and getting the result. Workers may be hired and fired; workers may be busy or waiting for something to do. Workers are highly specialized; some can do only integer addition; others can do only division. Workers responsible for complex tasks ask other workers specialized in appropriate subtasks for their assistance. No worker does more than one task at a time. If two or more commands are simultaneously directed to the same worker, that worker randomly selects and responds to one of them. A worker starts working when another worker asks him to do so, and he always responds to the one who commanded him.

Communication between workers is restricted to the passing of formal messages. Workers know only those workers who command them and those that they command. This knowledge can be gained only through messages. We are not interested in the physical time which is necessary for messages to arrive at their destination, and for tasks to be performed. We do assume however that this physical time is finite, and that every message is serviced in finite time after its arrival. The only point of interest is the before-after relationship between all the messages. A message is sent before a task is performed and before a response is returned. A task of evaluation is associated with every primitive statement and every operation invocation. A worker is associated with each task. Moreover, there is a worker assigned to each carrier declared (objects of type cell@ and derived types) and each instance of description used.

15.1.1. Context

Every worker has a special label called "context". The context is either his own name, or the name of the worker who hired him. Only a restricted category of workers has the privilege to give their name as context. These workers then always have their own name as context: in CONLAN, they correspond to instances of descriptions. The boss of the team, i.e the root description segment worker, is such a worker.

A worker gets his context when he is hired, and keeps it thereafter. This context is used as a parameter in some types of messages which may be sent to other workers. It serves to verify the access rights to carrier parameters of operations and descriptions.

15.1.2. Principles of Messages

There is a fixed number of categories of messages. Each category of messages is directed to, or emitted by, workers attached to a given category of segments. For instance, a COMPUTE message is always directed to a worker attached to a function, and a RESULT message is always emitted by such a worker when he returns the computed function result.

A message therefore includes a keyword, defining its category, possibly followed by one or more parameters. A message includes the name of the worker who sent it and his context when appropriate.

A parameter can either be readily understood by the worker who receives it, or be too complex and require the cooperation of other workers to evaluate it. Parameters that are immediately understood are constant denotations, and declared names of CONLAN objects. Parameters that require evaluation are expressions.

15.1.3. Objects

The existence of a universe of objects is assumed in the evaluation model. The objects of the model universe correspond to all the elements of primitive and defined types available in the language being modeled. In order to remove from the model a number of dynamic type checks, all objects of the model universe have a unique denotation, and no two objects have the same denotation.

In the model universe for CONLAN, as will be seen in more detail later, when no ambiguity exists, the CONLAN denotation is used for objects of types other than cell@. Booleans are written "true" and "false" in the model, to distinguish them from integer "0" and "1". Integers are written in decimal notation. Carriers, i.e., objects of type cell@ and derived types, are represented in the model universe by the name of their corresponding cell worker (see Section 15.2.2).

The objects of the model universe appear as parameters of exchanged messages. They are immediately recognizable by the workers who receive them. In the following, in order to distinguish them from CONLAN objects, they are written underlined.

15.1.4. Principles of Evaluation

In the following, we shall only consider pieces of CONLAN text that contain an operation invocation part, that is DESCRIPTION segments, ACTIVITY segments, and FUNCTION segments. CONLAN and TYPE segments only include a list of definitions; these two categories are statically evaluated (stage 1 below), and the result is the creation of sets of new objects and sets of new tasks. These segments are not subject to dynamic evaluation, which necessitates stages 2 and 3 below; their evaluation is therefore a special simplified case. Moreover, we shall consider that the root segment under evaluation is a DESCRIPTION segment.

Compiling this segment corresponds, in our model, to the creation of a team of workers for the task of evaluating the outer DESCRIPTION segment. The workers of the team represent the semantics of all segments and carriers in the DESCRIPTION.

The total number of workers varies during evaluation. Compile time actions correspond to hiring all workers who will be present during the whole evaluation process, and establishing their hierarchical links.

Messages are being exchanged when the hardware designer asks for an evaluation of his description. Two special workers, outside the hierarchical team, pre-exists:

- The "environment" worker serves as interface between the hardware designer and the team, interprets the evaluation commands, and acts as communication supervisor. The environment is responsible for sending the first message to the team boss to start the evaluation.

- The "recruiter" is capable of providing new workers when needed, and therefore receives all hiring requests.

15.1.4.1. Stage 1: Compile Time Actions

The DESCRIPTION segment is written in a given CONLAN language member. For that language, tasks of evaluation and workers capable of executing them pre-exist for all DESCRIPTION segments, FUNCTION segments, and ACTIVITY segments known in the language. For every new segment defined by the text to be evaluated, an additional task is created. The outer DESCRIPTION segment is one such task; others are all locally defined DESCRIPTION, FUNCTION, and ACTIVITY segments. A worker is hired and attached to the outer DESCRIPTION segment. This worker is made the boss of a team of workers who are hired for the entire evaluation process. This team of permanent workers includes:

- one worker for each declared carrier within the scope of this description, including interface carriers. At this point, synonymies are resolved and declaration inconsistencies (unknown type designations, name conflicts, etc...) result in an error report.

- one worker for each instance of description used, if any. As above, errors in USE statements (unknown description designators, incorrect actual attributes, name conflicts, etc...) are reported.

- one worker for each occurrence of a STATIC function or activity invocation in the BODY part of the description.

In addition, the description worker is made aware of all the tasks to be performed and of the existence of workers capable of evaluating all the dynamic operations invoked in his BODY part. It will be his privilege to hire and fire those workers during subsequent stages.

In turn, each worker attached to a STATIC operation and to an instance of a description is made the boss of his own team of permanent workers. The hiring process is repeated until each newly hired worker corresponds to a carrier. It should be noted that only permanently active workers are hired during this stage. In particular, workers associated with dynamic function and activity invocations do not belong to this permanent team. In addition, during this phase a unique operation definition is identified for each operation invocation that appears in the text under evaluation. Reference to parameter types may be necessary; the author of the text is responsible for eliminating ambiguities, of course. Errors such as invocation of an undefined operation or the wrong number of parameters are reported. All invocations are transformed to prefix notation using the unique names. Description workers are made aware of these identifiers so that they may later hire appropriate workers.

ATT actual parameters of all segments are evaluated: if the evaluation is not possible at this stage, or if the result is not in accordance with the formal type designator, an error is reported; otherwise, the result of this evaluation is used to select the appropriate task (description instantiation, function or activity invocation) or type of objects (reference to a generic type). Thus, the results of ATT actual parameter evaluations appear in hiring requests sent to the recruiter.

Objects imported in an operation through an IMPORT statement are treated as additional

- formal parameters at the point of the operation definition

- actual parameters at the point of the operation invocation.

If no error occurs, stage 2 is initiated.

15.1.4.2. Stage 2: Activity Parameter Evaluation
Upon receipt of an initiating message from the environment the team leader

- sends to the recruiter a set of messages to hire all necessary temporary workers, one per local dynamic activity invocation.

- when all hired workers are received, sends to each worker associated to a subtask an initiating message. All are instructed simultaneously to evaluate the actual parameters of their invocation.

The process is recursively repeated, down the hierarchy of workers, until workers associated to elementary tasks have been initiated.

Parameter evaluation may require hiring of workers attached to functions (when actual parameters are expressions) or to activities (invoked as alternatives of conditional statements). All activities are required to return a "done" acknowledgement when they have evaluated all their parameters and successfully initiated all their subtasks, if any. Thus, a worker, responsible for a complex task, once all subtasks have been initiated, waits for all acknowledgements before returning the "done" message to his caller.

If a parameter is not recognized by an activity, or if an error has been found by a subtask, that activity returns an "error" message. "Done" or "error" messages climb up the hirarchy of workers in reverse order of initiating messages. When all activity workers have responded, and none of them has sent an error message, stage 3 is initiated.

15.1.4.3. Stage 3: Activity Execution

According to the same procedure as above, all activity workers are sent a "start" message; they return "done" when they have terminated.

A worker responsible for an elementary task performs his task directly, and responds to the one who commanded him. A worker responsible for a complex task, once all subtakes have been started, waits until all answers have been received. If at least one answer is an error message, an error is answered to the one who commanded the task. Otherwise, after additional checks when necessary, the worker fires all temporary workers that he commanded, and gives a positive answer to the one who commanded the task. Answer messages are transmitted back along the hierarchy, up to the team boss. This is the end of one pass of evaluation of the text.

One pass constitutes the complete evaluation of a pscl text, and one step of the evaluation of a bcl text. If more steps are required, evaluation resumes at stage 2.

Rule: A step of evaluation has no error if it contains no error message.

An equivalent statement is: A step of evaluation has no error if the team boss has no error message for this step.

The following sections develop this model of evaluation. Starting from evaluation of the operations given in Primitive Set CONLAN, the evaluation of user defined segments is constructed. In a later chapter it is shown how the interpretation of a description at the BASE CONLAN level is derived from the pscl level.

15.2. The Worker Model of Evaluation

15.2.1. Messages

A message is a 4-tuple in which the second and fourth components may be empty.

(worker_name, context, keyword, parameter_list)

We will use an informal notation to write messages.

worker_name: context, keyword(parameter_list)

where worker_name is the name of the sender of the message, and context is the name of the worker who hired the sender or the sender's own name if he is a description worker. The context part is not necessary on all messages, and in the following we shall indicate it only when its presence is required. When the context component is not required, messages will be expressed with the notation:

worker_name: keyword(parameter_list)

If the parameter list is empty we abbreviate further.

worker_name: keyword

At the pscl level, an operation or description worker w may originate the following types of messages with context c:

Message   Meaning

w: c, EVAL(p1, p2, ... pn)
                 directs an activity or description worker to evaluate its actual parameters.

w: EVALUATED
                 answer of an activity or description worker who has successfully evaluated all actual parameters.

w: START   directs an activity or description worker to perform the task described by the corresponding segment body.

w: DONE   answer of an activity or description worker who has completed its evaluation task without error.

w: COMPUTE(p1, p2, ... pi)
                 directs a function worker to evaluate its actual parameters, its body (if any) and its return expression.

w: RESULT(r)   answer of a function worker where 'r' is the result of the computation.

w: ERROR(explanation)
                 answer of a worker who has encountered an error condition in performing its task. This message can replace EVALUATED, DONE or RESULT(r). The parameter "explanation" is an element of type string that explains the reason of the failure. String "explanation" may be empty, or a very sophisticated sentence, depending upon the implementation.

w: RECEIVE(cell_worker_name)

         passes an interface carrier to an inner description worker.

In messages EVAL and COMPUTE, the pi are the actual parameters of the operation. An actual parameter can be:

- a constant,

- a worker name, corresponding to a declared object,

- an expression

Messages are also exchanged between operation segments and the recruiter, in order to (1) hire a worker for an internal operation (nested invocations) or (2) get a fresh carrier (local declarations of carriers in operation segments). Such messages take the following forms:

Message   Meaning

w: SEND(operation_designator)   request to the recruiter to provide a worker for the operation specified.

w: SEND(type_designator)   request to the recruiter to provide a fresh carrier of the type specified, and its attached worker.

recruiter: RECEIVE(worker_name)   answer of the recruiter, which provides the requested worker.

Other messages, with keywords EMPTY, GET, PUT, PERMIT or FORBID are requests exclusively addressed to cell workers, and will be explained in the appropriate section.

In the following, to shorten the text, we shall write "function plus", or "plus", instead of "the worker attached to function plus". Further, the transmission of messages will be denoted with an arrow with the receiver of the message identified at the point.

w1: message -> w2   is to be interpreted as 'w2 receives "message" from w1'.
w1 <- w2: message   is to be interpreted as 'w1 receives "message" from w2'.

The second form is the preferred expression of a returned object, or an acknowledgement.

To represent a set of messages, we shall make a distinction between concurrent and sequential exchanges. The following format indicates concurrent messages:

```
w1: message1 -> wr1
w2: message2 -> wr2
w3: message3 -> wr3
.....
wn: messagen -> wrn
```

whereas sequential messages are indicated by:

```
w1: message1 -> wr1
   +
w2: message2 -> wr2
   +
w3: message3 -> wr3
   +
.....
   +
wn: messagen -> wrn
```

15.2.2. Behavior of Cells, and their Specific Messages

15.2.2.1. Access Rights
A cell can appear in three different positions:

1. Local to an instance of a DESCRIPTION segment. The cell identifier appears in a DECLARE statement, in the BODY of the DESCRIPTION. Such a cell can be read as well as modified, using invocations of get@ and put@ in the operation invocation part of the DESCRIPTION.

2. At the interface of an instance of DESCRIPTION. The cell identifier appears in the interface list, and is under the scope of an IN, OUT, or INOUT keyword. The cell can be accessed both in the segment of which it is an interface element, and in the enclosing segment, if any. Moreover, the USE statement of the enclosing segment may indicate synonymy with an interface element of one or several other instances of DESCRIPTION segments: Then a single cell can be referenced in several instances of DESCRIPTION segments. The IN, OUT, INOUT specifications in each segment definition indicate which instances can modify the cell content, through invocation of put@, and which ones only have a read access.

3. Local to an ACTIVITY or FUNCTION segment. The cell is either declared in the BODY or appears as a formal parameter of the operation segment. Such a cell is unknown to any segment that invokes the operation segment of the cell.

Cells in categories 1) and 2) are permanent for the whole duration of the description evaluation. In addition, these cells are known to the environment, which can read and write into them. Cells in category 3) are present as long as the worker attached to their owner operation segment is present. Once they have been hired by this operation, the environment has no access to them.

The access right to a cell is defined by the set of workers which may have knowledge of the cell worker name. The passing of this name through messages is supposed to take place in accordance with the importing and exporting rules of the corresponding segment. This can be checked statically at compile time. The right to modify a cell can also be verified statically and is only modelled dynamically for the sake of clarity.

This variety of positions and access rights to be modelled, which is a super-set of those commonly found in CHDL's, motivated the following definition of the cell worker, which represents the semantics of carriers in a description.

15.2.2.2. Nature of a Cell

A cell consists of the following three items:

- The type of its content. A cell may only contain objects of a given type. The type of a cell is fixed when that cell is created, and cannot be changed thereafter.

- Its content, which is initially empty

- Its capability. The capability is a locking mechanism. It is an unordered set of worker names, which may include the environment. Only those workers who are named in the capability have a right to modify the content of the cell. The initial capability of a cell, consisting of the name of the requesting worker, is provided by the recruiter, when a worker is hired for that cell, and can be changed thereafter by PERMIT and FORBID messages.

The content and capability of a cell are under the control of the worker attached to the cell, who modifies them in response to the messages he receives.

For any segment, and for every type defined in its reference language or in the segment itself, an infinite number of cells able to contain an element of that type exist (conceptually). When a new type is defined, compile time actions include creation of all the elements of that type, and creation of a mechanism, given to the recruiter, to obtain cells which may accept those elements as content.

15.2.2.3. Exchange of Messages with a Cell Worker

Let 'w' be the name of any worker, 'cw' be the name of a worker attached to a cell, and 'id' be the name of the context of 'w'. 'cw' is capable of understanding a number of messages emitted by 'w'; the effect of their reception is defined below.

Testing for an Empty Cell

        w: EMPTY -> cw
            +
        w <- cw: RESULT(r)

Upon receipt of the EMPTY message, cw returns a RESULT message with r = <u>true</u> if the cell is empty, and r = <u>false</u> otherwise.

Asking for the Content of a Cell

```
w: GET -> cw
    +
w <- cw: RESULT(r)
or
w: GET -> cw
    +
w <- cw: ERROR('empty cell')
```

Upon receipt of the GET message, cw returns a RESULT message with its content r if its cell is not empty, and an ERROR message if its cell is empty.

Writing into a Cell

```
w: PUT(u) -> cw
    +
w <- cw: DONE
or
w: PUT(u) -> cw
    +
w <- cw: ERROR(explanation)
```

Upon receipt of the PUT message, which includes the new content being requested, cw performs 2 tests that must be passed before the content of the cell is changed.

- If 'w' does not belong to the capability, writing is not allowed in this context, and an ERROR message is returned.

- If u is not an element of the content-type of the cell, an ERROR message is returned.

Otherwise, cw removes the previous content of the cell, if it was not empty, and puts u into the cell. Then a DONE message is returned.

Adding a Name to the Capability

```
w: id, PERMIT -> cw     (if id = w or id in capability)
    +
w <- cw: DONE
or
w: id, PERMIT -> cw     (if id ~ = w and id not in capability)
    +
w <- cw: ERROR('write access not allowed')
```

Upon receipt of the PERMIT message, cw compares the sender's name and context. If they are identical or the context belongs to the capability, the sender's name w is added to the capability, otherwise an ERROR message is returned.

Removing a Name from the Capability

> w: FORBID -> cw   (if w in capability)
>   +
> w <- cw: DONE
> or
> w: FORBID -> c   (if w not in capability)
>   +
> w <- cw: ERROR('write access still not allowed')

Upon receipt of the FORBID message, cw checks if the sender's name belongs to the capability of cw. If this is true, the sender's name is removed from the capability, otherwise an ERROR message is returned.

15.2.3. Behavior of Operation Workers

Operation workers model the evaluation of ACTIVITY and FUNCTION segments. Although ACTIVITY and FUNCTION workers communicate with an invoking worker by specific messages, they have common rules for getting local cells, hiring workers for nested operations, and evaluating their parameters.

15.2.3.1. Hiring Local cell and Operation Workers

Cells local to an operation have a life time

- limited to the duration of a single execution of the operation, if it is DYNAMIC; then each invocation of the operation is independent of the previous one (a necessity for recursion)

- equal to the life time of the enclosing description if the operations is STATIC; then previous invocations may have an influence on the effect of a following one (as in random number generators).

STATIC and DYNAMIC operations differ by their mode of hiring local cell and operation workers.

For a STATIC operation, an initialization phase takes place, before any received message is taken into account. A group of messages is exchanged once and for all with the recruiter, in order to hire

- one cell worker for each carrier declared in the operation body,

- one operation worker for each invocation of a STATIC operation.

Each operation worker hired at this point in turn performs his own initialization phase, and the process is repeated down the tree of nested STATIC operation invocations. All these workers will have the same life time as the STATIC operation that hired them.

For a DYNAMIC operation, no such initialization takes place. Messages are exchanged with the recruiter, at the beginning of each evaluation, in order to hire one cell worker for each carrier declared in the operation body. The life time of these workers does not exceed the duration of the operation evaluation. A DYNAMIC operation may not invoke a STATIC one.

15.2.3.2. Characterization of Operation Worker

When a worker w is hired for an operation evaluation by a SEND message issued to the recruiter by his caller, this worker is assigned his callers's name w, which was indicated on the SEND message, as context.

Let 'w' be an invoking worker, 'c' its context, 'fw' an invoked function worker, 'aw' an invoked activity worker.

A FUNCTION worker has a single exchange of messages with the worker w who commands his evaluation:

> w: COMPUTE(p1, p2, ...pn) -> fw
> +
>   "evaluation of the parameters"
> +
>   "execution of the function body"
> +
>   "evaluation of the function result"
> +
> w <- fw: RESULT(result)

An ACTIVITY worker has a double exchange of messages with the worker who commanded his evaluation: an intermediate answer is sent after the parameters have been evaluated, and a new message is necessary to start the evaluation of the body:

> w: c, EVAL(p1, p2, ...pm) -> aw
> +
>   "evaluation of the parameters"
> +
> w <- aw: EVALUATED
> +
> w: START -> aw
> +
>   "execution of the activity body"
> +
> w <- aw: DONE

15.2.3.3. Parameter Evaluation

The parameters attached to COMPUTE and EVAL messages are position parameters which, in CONLAN, correspond to the non-ATTRIBUTE formal parameters of the operation followed by the list of imported objects.

The worker attached to a function (activity) knows a COMPUTE (EVAL) "message skeleton", which indicates the number and types of expected parameters for acceptable messages.

Parameter evaluation has to be done by:

- a function worker, receiving a COMPUTE message

- an activity worker, receiving an EVAL message

Each actual parameter is matched against the corresponding typed formal element in the parameter list of the COMPUTE or EVAL skeleton. Then the following actions are carried out:

(i) For all actual parameters which are expressions, appropriate function workers are hired and COMPUTE messages are sent to them concurrently.

(ii) When the RESULT messages have been received, or if the actual parameters are constants or worker names, the types of the actual parameters are verified that they are of the expected types.

(iii) If a formal parameter is a carrier with W access right (activities only) the actual parameter (cell worker) is sent a PERMIT message.

These standard actions for the evaluation of parameters may be complemented by additional actions, to express the special semantics of parameter passing (i.e., invocation of special write protection operations) depending on the particular language.

15.2.3.4. Evaluation of an Operation BODY

If the BODY of an operation has a nonempty operation invocation part, then it amounts to a list of conditional or unconditional, primitive or user-defined, activity invocations. The principles of evaluating these concurrent invocations in the worker model are now explained. A worker is hired, for each invocation of a DYNAMIC activity. This means in particular that if the same activity "abc" is invoked 3 times in the operation body, 3 "abc" workers are hired. Then, each "active" worker, i.e., under the scope of a true condition (determined by a SELECT conditional form) or unconditionally invoked, is sent an EVAL message, with his actual parameters. All EVAL messages are sent concurrently. If at least one ERROR message replaces an expected EVALUATED message, an ERROR message is sent to the caller, and the evaluation of the operation body is stopped. Otherwise, when all invoked activity workers have transmitted their EVALUATED message, each of them is sent a START message. ALL START message are sent concurrently. Once again, if at least one ERROR message replaces an expected DONE message, an ERROR message is sent to the caller, and the evaluation of the operation is stopped. Otherwise, when all invoked activity workers have transmitted their DONE message, the evaluation of the BODY part is completed. For ACTIVITYs, this is also the end of the operation evaluation, and a DONE message is sent to the caller. Before this is done, the cell worker which corresponds to formal parameter with W access right are sent a FORBID message. In the case of functions, the RETURN expression must be computed before a RESULT message is sent to the caller. The model of the evaluation of an operation BODY can be decribed as follows, where act1, act2,..., actn represent the active internal activity workers out of which j are dynamic (for simplicity, we assume that all invocations are unconditional), and op and opctxt represent the operation being evaluated and its context:

" start of the operation BODY evaluation "
" hiring activity workers "
op: SEND(activity1) -> recruiter
        +
op <- recruiter: RECEIVE(act1)
        +
op: SEND(activity2) -> recruiter
        +
op <- recruiter: RECEIVE(act2)
        +
        ......

        +
op: SEND(activityj) -> recruiter
        +
op <- recruiter: RECEIVE(actj)
        +
" inner activities: parameter evaluation stage "
op: opctxt, EVAL(p11, p12,...p1m1) -> act1
op: opctxt, EVAL(p21, p22,...p2m2) -> act2
        ......

op: opctxt, EVAL(pn1, pn2,...pnmn) -> actn
        +
op <- act1: EVALUATED
op <- act2: EVALUATED
        ......

op <- actn: EVALUATED
        +
" inner activities: body evaluation stage "
op: START -> act1
op: START -> act2
        .....

op: START -> actn
        +
op <- act1: DONE
op <- act2: DONE
        .....

op <- actn: DONE
        " end of operation BODY evaluation "

15.2.4. Behavior of DESCRIPTION Workers

A DESCRIPTION worker models a digital system with fixed structure. There is always a non empty initialization phase, during which all interface and local carriers are obtained. A DESCRIPTION can be divided into an arbitrary number of simpler nested descriptions: this structure is reflected in the initialization phase, during which a worker is hired for each nested instance of description.

The main property of a DESCRIPTION worker is that he transmits activation and answer messages to the next level in the hierarchy of description and operation workers, and that he fixes his own name as context of his messages. These messages are EVAL-EVALUATED and START-DONE pairs, as for ACTIVITY workers.

A DESCRIPTION evaluation task can therefore be decomposed into three stages:

- initialization

- EVAL-EVALUATED stage

- START-DONE stage

15.2.4.1. Initialization

The initialization stage of a DESCRIPTION evaluation is divided into 4 parts, out of which two may be empty.

1. All cell workers, corresponding to the interface carriers of the DESCRIPTION, are first received. If the DESCRIPTION worker is associated with the outermost (root) DESCRIPTION segment, i.e., is the boss of the team, his interface elements are being sent to him by the environment; otherwise, they are sent by the worker of the enclosing DESCRIPTION segment. The DESCRIPTION worker sends a PERMIT message to each cell worker who stands for a modifiable interface element (declared INOUT or OUT in a CONLAN text).

2. If the DESCRIPTION segment contains nested instances of DESCRIPTION segments, a worker is hired for each nested instance.

3. A worker is hired for each invocation of a STATIC operation. A cell worker is hired for each carrier declared in the BODY of the DESCRIPTION, including interface carriers of nested instances of DESCRIPTION segments. Synonymies are taken care of at this stage (Section 11.3). A FORBID message is sent to each cell worker who stands for an interface element of a nested instance which may not be modified outside that instance (declared OUT in CONLAN).

4. If point 2 is non-empty, each worker hired for a nested instance of DESCRIPTION is sent his interface cell workers.

Remark: The capability of a cell worker a priori contains the name of the worker who hired him. PERMIT messages sent to an interface cell have the effect of adding to his capability the names of all workers who may modify the cell content. A FORBID message removes from his capability the name of the worker who hired him, if this worker may not modify the cell content.

15.2.4.2. EVAL-EVALUATED Phase

DESCRIPTION evaluation is initiated by the reception of an EVAL message with actual parameters, that correspond to the formal non-carrier parameters of the DESCRIPTION. An appropriate function worker is hired for each of these actual parameters that is an expression, and COMPUTE messages are sent to them concurrently. When the result messages have been received, or if the actual parameters are constants, their types are verified. Then a worker is hired for each invocation of a dynamic operation in the description BODY. Then the DESCRIPTION worker sends concurrently an EVAL message, with actual parameters, to each invoked activity, and an EVAL message without parameters to each nested instance of description. All EVAL messages have this DESCRIPTION worker's name as context. Then the DESCRIPTION worker waits for all answers.

If at least one ERROR message is received, the dynamic operation workers who had been hired during this phase are fired, and an ERROR message is sent to the initiating worker. Otherwise, an EVALUATED message is issued, and the DESCRIPTION worker waits for the START message.

15.2.4.3. START-DONE Phase

Upon receipt of the START message, the DESCRIPTION worker sends concurrently START messages to all invoked activity workers and to all description workers of the next level of nesting, and waits for all answers.

When all answers are received, the dynamic operation workers who had been hired during the previous phase are fired. If at least one ERROR message replaces an expected DONE message, an ERROR message is sent back, otherwise a DONE message is answered to the worker who commanded the DESCRIPTION evaluation.

Remark: The DESCRIPTION worker of the outer DESCRIPTION segment is the boss of the team of workers, and his EVAL-EVALUATED and START-DONE communications are exchanged with the environment.

15.3. The Semantics of Pscl in Terms of the Worker Model

Defining the semantic of pscl using the worker model is done by

- chosing the primitive types of pscl as the universe of object for the model

- defining the behavior of the workers which are associated to the primitive carriers, operations and statements.

- specifying, how segment definitions and usage are translated into the model.

15.3.1. The Universe of Primitive Objects

The model universe of objects for pscl includes:

- the integers, in decimal notation

- the booleans, denoted <u>true</u> and <u>false</u>

- the character strings, quoted

- the fully qualified designators of known types

- the unique names of all cell workers

- the finite sequences of objects (i.e. tuples) of the universe

15.3.2. Primitive Functions on Types other than cell@.

Functions and operations listed in table 13-1 of the report are the subject of this paragraph. A predefined function evaluation task, identified with the function name prefixed with the corresponding type name, is associated to each one of these functions.

When a primitve function receives a COMPUTE message, it evaluate its parameters. If no error condition exists, it returns the element of its range that it computes as the single parameter of a RESULT message. The mechanism by which the result is obtained is not described here, since no formal definition of a primitive function is provided. For instance:

$$w: COMPUTE(\underline{0,1}) \text{ -> int.equal}$$
$$+$$
$$w \text{ <- int.equal: RESULT}(\underline{false})$$

If an error condition is found, either in evaluating the parameters, or because an assertion about a parameter is not fulfilled, an ERROR message is returned. For instance:

$$w: COMPUTE((.\underline{1,10,23}.),\underline{4}) \text{ -> tuple@.select@}$$
$$+$$
$$w \text{ <- tuple@.select@: ERROR('position greater than size').}$$

In the following, when no ambiguity exist, the type prefix of the function name will be omitted.

15.3.3. Primitive Operations on Type Cell@

A cell worker is attached to each cell in a description, or operation segment written in pscl. As a short hand notation, this worker will be referred to by the cell identifier, and we shall make no distinction between a cell and the worker attached to it. A cell is capable of interpreting several messages, corresponding to the primitive operations defined on cells.

15.3.3.1. Function empty@

Invocation of empty@(x) in a CONLAN text results in the transmission:

$$w: COMPUTE(x) \text{ -> empty@}$$

Parameter x is evaluated. If evaluation of x does not yield a declared cell, an error condition exists, and an ERROR message is returned to the caller. Otherwise, an EMPTY message is sent to x.

$$\text{empty@: EMPTY -> x}$$

x recognizes this message, and returns to empty@ the message

$$\text{empty@ <- x: RESULT(r)}$$

where r is <u>true</u> if the cell is empty, <u>false</u> otherwise. The RESULT message is propagated by empty@ to its caller.

15.3.3.2. Function get@

Invocation of cell@.get@(x) in a CONLAN text results in sending the message:

$$\text{w: COMPUTE(x) -> get@}$$

Parameter x is evaluated. If evaluation of x does not yield a declared cell, an error condition exists, and an ERROR message is sent to the caller. Otherwise, a GET message is sent to x.

$$\text{get@: GET -> x}$$

x recognizes this message, and returns

$$\text{get@ <- x: ERROR('empty cell')}$$

if the cell is empty and

$$\text{get@ <- x: RESULT(r)}$$

where r is the content of x, if the cell is not empty. The received message is propagated by get@ to its caller.

15.3.3.3. Operation put@

Invocation of put@(x, u) in a CONLAN text results in an exchange of messages. Upon receipt of

$$\text{w: id, EVAL(x, u) -> put@}$$

parameters x and u are evaluated. If evaluation of x does not yield a declared cell, an error condition exists, and an ERROR message is returned to the caller. Then a PERMIT message is sent to the cell worker:

$$\text{put@: w,PERMIT -> x}$$

Upon receipt of

$$\text{put@ <- x: DONE}$$

the results of the parameter evaluations are kept, and an EVALUATED message is returned to the caller:

$$\text{w <- put@: EVALUATED}$$

Otherwise, if w does not belong to the capability of x, an ERROR message is returned

$$\text{put@ <- x: ERROR('write access not allowed')}$$

which is passed on to the caller w of put@.

Upon receipt of

$$\text{w: START -> put@}$$

put@ sends a PUT message to x.

$$\text{put@: PUT(\underline{u}) -> x}$$

When x receives the message and if u̲ is an element of the content-type of the cell, u̲ becomes its new content, and a DONE message is̲ returned. Otherwise, an ERROR message is returned. Before this message is propagated by put@ to its caller, put@ removes its name from the capability of x:

$$put@ \; \langle\text{-} \; x: DONE$$
$$+$$
$$put@: FORBID \; \text{-}\rangle \; x$$
$$+$$
$$put@ \; \langle\text{-} \; x: DONE$$
$$+$$
$$w \; \langle\text{-} \; put@: DONE$$

or

$$put@ \; \langle\text{-} \; x: ERROR('wrong content type')$$
$$+$$
$$put@: FORBID \; \text{-}\rangle \; x$$
$$+$$
$$put@ \; \langle\text{-} \; x: DONE$$
$$+$$
$$w \; \langle\text{-} \; put@: ERROR('wrong content type')$$

15.3.4. Conditional Expressions

15.3.4.1. IF Conditional Expression

Let 'be' symbolize a boolean expression, and 'a' and 'b' symbolize two expressions. The statement

$$IF \; be \; THEN \; a \; ELSE \; b \; ENDIF$$

is evaluated when its attached worker receives the message

$$w: COMPUTE(be, a, b) \; \text{-}\rangle \; IF$$

The evaluation is done in two steps.

1. Evaluation of the condition. The first parameter is evaluated. If the result is not an element of type bool, an error condition exists.

2. Evaluation of the result. If the first step was successful, depending on the value of 'be', the second or the third parameter is evaluated.

If 'be' is true, 'a' is evaluated, otherwise, 'b' is evaluated. The resulting value (or error condition) of this evaluation is the result of the whole conditional expression.

The statement

$$IF \; be1 \; THEN \; a1 \; ELIF \; be2 \; THEN \; a2 \; ELIF \; ... \; ELSE \; an \; ENDIF$$

is transformed into

IF be1 THEN a1 ELSE IF be2 THEN a2 ELSE IF .... ENDIF ENDIF... ENDIF

Processing is then done according to the usual rules applied to nested function invocations. If for instance be1 is _false_ and bc2 is _true_, the following exchanges of COMPUTE and RESULT messages will take place:

w: COMPUTE(be1, a1, IF be2 THEN a2 ELSE IF...ENDIF) -> IF_1

+

IF_1: COMPUTE(be2, a2, IF be3 THEN a3 ELSE...ENDIF) -> IF_2

+

IF_1 <- IF_2: RESULT(va2)

+

w <- IF_1: RESULT(va2)

Note that two different workers , represented above by IF_1 and IF_2, are necessary to evaluate two nested IF conditionals.

15.3.4.2. CASE Conditional Expression

Let 'x' be an expression returning objects of a given type, 'x1','x2',...'xn' be the denotation or declared identifiers of n different elements of that type, and 'e1','e2',...'en','en+1' be n+1 expressions. For the conditional expression:

CASE x IS
    x1 : e1;
    x2 : e2;
    ....
    xn : en;
    ELSE en+1;
ENDCASE

A worker CASE, capable of interpreting a CASE statement with n cases and an additional ELSE clause, is hired. The statement is evaluated when its attached worker receives the message

w: COMPUTE(x, x1, e1, x2, e2, ...xn, en, en+1) -> CASE

The evaluation is done in two steps.

1. Evaluation of the selecting expression. The first parameter, 'x', is evaluated. This may require hiring of other workers, and induce further exchange of messages. If evaluation of 'x' results in an error message, CASE relays that message back to its caller. Otherwise, the result is an element of the expected type.

2. Evaluation of the result. If evaluation of 'x' has not resulted in an error report, the obtained value is compared with 'x1', 'x2',...'xn'. If equality with one of the 'xi' is found, the corresponding 'ei' is selected, otherwise 'en+1' is selected.

The selected expression is in turn evaluated, by hiring the appropriate worker, and sending it a COMPUTE message. The resulting value, or error condition, is the result of the whole CASE expression.

If the ELSE part of the CASE conditional is omitted, and 'x'evaluates to none of the 'xi', an error is reported.

15.3.5. Predicate, Element and Subset Constructors

15.3.5.1. FORALL@ Predicate
The statement

$$\text{FORALL@ x: atype IS pred(x,a,b,...) ENDFOR}$$

is evaluated when its attached worker receives the message

$$\text{w: COMPUTE(x, atype, pred(x,a,b,...))} \rightarrow \text{FORALL@}$$

The evaluation is done in two steps.

1. <u>Parameter Recognition</u> The first parameter is always recognized. The second parameter must be a valid type designator, else an error condition exists. The third parameter, translated to prefix notation, must result in a call to a function with boolean range, else an error condition exists.

2. <u>Predicate Evaluation</u> This second step is started only if no error was found in the previous one. If atype is empty, then the FORALL@ worker directly returns <u>true</u>. If atype is not empty, and pred (x,a,b,...) evaluates to <u>true</u> for every z in atype, then the FORALL@ worker returns <u>true</u>. If the predicate evaluation returns an ERROR for least one element of atype, then evaluation of the FORALL@ statement results in an error report. If no error occurs, and pred (x,a,b,...) evaluates to <u>false</u> for at least one element of atype, then the FORALL@ worker returns <u>false</u>. The mechanism by which pred (x,a,b,...) is evaluated for all the elements of atype is implied.

15.3.5.2. FORSOME@ Predicate
The statement

$$\text{FORSOME@ x: atype IS pred(x,a,b,...) ENDFOR}$$

is evaluated in the same way as the FORALL@ predicate with the exception of the test on the results returned by the predicate.

If atype is empty, then the FORSOME@ worker directly returns <u>false</u>.

In the absence of error, if pred (x,a,b,...) evaluates to <u>true</u> for at least one x in atype, then the FORSOME@ worker returns <u>true</u>, otherwise it returns <u>false</u>.

15.3.5.3. FORONE@ Predicate
The statement:

$$\text{FORONE@ x: atype IS pred(x,a,b,...) ENDFOR}$$

is evaluated in the same way as the FORALL@ predicate with the exception of the test on the results returned by the predicate.

If atype is empty, then the FORONE@ worker directly returns <u>false</u>.

In the absence of error, if pred (x,a,b,...) evaluates to <u>true</u> for exactly one x in atype, then the FORONE@ worker returns <u>true</u>, otherwise it returns <u>false</u>.

15.3.5.4. THE@ Constructor
The statement

$$\text{THE@ x: atype WITH pred(x,a,b,...) ENDTHE}$$

is evaluated when its attached worker receives the message

$$\text{w: COMPUTE(x, atype, pred(x,a,b,...)) -> THE@}$$

Parameters are recognized as for FORALL@ statements. Then, if no error was found in parameter recognition, the THE@ evaluation begins. If atype is empty, or if pred (x,a,b,...) evaluates to <u>true</u> for zero or more than one element of atype, then an error condition exists. Otherwise, the unique element of atype for which pred evaluates to <u>true</u> is returned as the result of the THE@ worker.

15.3.5.5. ALL Constructor
The statement

$$\text{ALL x: atype WITH pred(x,a,b,...) ENDALL}$$

is evaluated when its attached worker receives the message

$$\text{w: COMPUTE(x, atype, pred(x,a,b,...)) -> ALL}$$

The evaluation is done in two steps. Parameters are recognized as for FORALL@ statements. Then, if no error was found in parameter recognition, ALL evaluation begins. If atype is empty, the empty set is returned. If an error is found while evaluating pred, an ERROR message is returned. Otherwise, ALL returns a RESULT message with the (possibly empty) subset of elements of atype for which pred evaluates to <u>true</u>.

15.3.6. Primitive Conditional Activity Invocations
The operation invocation part of a CONLAN segment is a list of activity invocations. We have seen before that invocation of the most primitive activity, operation put@ on cells, amounts to a sequence of exchanges of messages (when no error is found):

$$\text{w: id, EVAL(parameters) -> put@}$$
$$+$$
$$\text{w <- put@: EVALUATED}$$
$$+$$
$$\text{w: START -> put@}$$
$$+$$
$$\text{w <- put@: DONE}$$

This sequence is general: it applies to every activity invocation, whether it be an invocation of put@, of a user-defined activity, or of a conditional form. Conditional forms are not activities themselves, they are a means to select activity invocations. Their effect is to transmit back and forth the messages between the selected invocations and their surrounding segment. We are now going to see in more details how they are interpreted.

15.3.6.1. IF Conditional

Let 'be' symbolize a boolean expression, and 'la1' and 'la2' two lists of activity invocations. The invocation of:

IF be THEN la1 ELSE la2 ENDIF

is evaluated by a worker attached to AIF (Activity IF, different from the expression IF), to which EVAL and START messages are directed.

Parameter Evaluation

Upon receipt of the message

w: id, EVAL(be, la1, la2) -> AIF

AIF hires a worker capable of interpreting expression be, put in prefix notation, and sends a COMPUTE message to that worker.

AIF: COMPUTE(be) -> wbe

If wbe returns an ERROR message, or a result different from true or false, that message is propagated. If wbe returns true, AIF takes its second parameter la1 into consideration and remembers the fact. If wbe returns false, AIF remembers that fact and takes its third parameter into consideration. Let us suppose la1 has been selected. Things would proceed identically for la2. If la1 is empty, an EVALUATED message is returned by AIF to its caller. If la1 is not empty, AIF hires a worker for each dynamic activity invocation in the list, and sends EVAL messages to.all the workers in the list. AIF always puts the context of its caller (i.e. 'id'), which it got through the EVAL message, on its request. This has the effect that a worker hired by AIF sees the outer 'non-AIF' worker as its context. All messages are sent concurrently. If at least one of the activities in la1 replies an ERROR message, an ERROR message is returned by AIF. Otherwise, when all activities in la1 have returned an EVALUATED message, AIF returns an EVALUATED message to its caller.

Activity Execution

Upon receipt of the message:

w: START -> AIF

AIF checks which activity list was selected during parameter evaluation. Let's assume again it was la1. If la1 is empty, a DONE message is returned by AIF. If la1 is not empty, AIF issues a START message toward each activity in the list. All messages are sent concurrently. If at least one of the activities in la1 replies with an ERROR message, an ERROR message is returned by AIF. Otherwise, when all activities in la1 have returned a DONE message, AIF returns a DONE message to its caller. Then all workers who have been hired during parameter evaluation are fired.

Invocation of

IF be THEN la1 ENDIF

corresponds to invocation of the standard

$$\text{IF bc THEN la1 ELSE la2 ENDIF}$$

with an empty la2. Invocation of

$$\text{IF be1 THEN la1 ELIF be2 THEN la2 ELSE la3 ENDIF}$$

is transformed into

$$\text{IF be1 THEN la1 ELSE IF be2 THEN la2 ELSE la3 ENDIF ENDIF}$$

and is processed as two nested standard IF conditionals to which two distinct workers must be associated. The same applies when more than one ELIF part is written.

15.3.6.2. CASE Conditional

Interpretation of the CASE conditional is based on the same principles as that of IF for activities (AIF). Invocation of:

```
CASE x IS
    x1 : la1 ;
    x2 : la2 ;
    .....
    xn : lan ;
    ELSE lan+1 ;
ENDCASE
```

is evaluated by a worker attached to ACASE (Activity CASE, different from the expression CASE). This evaluation is again done in two steps.

Parameter Evaluation

$$\text{w: id, EVAL(x, x1, la1, x2, la2, ... xn, lan, lan+1) -> ACASE}$$

Evaluation of x first takes place, possibly by hiring an appropriate function worker and sending him a COMPUTE message. If evaluation of x does not result in an error report, the obtained value is compared with x1, x2, ... xn. If equality with one of the xi is found, the corresponding activity list lai is selected, otherwise lan+1 is selected. If the selected list is not empty, a worker is hired for each dynamic activity invocation; EVAL messages are concurrently sent to every worker in the list. As in AIF the worker ACASE always puts the context of its caller, which it got through the EVAL message, on its requests. When all EVALUATED messages have been received, or if the list is empty, an EVALUATED message is sent by ACASE to its caller. If at least one ERROR message is received by ACASE, an ERROR message is issued instead.

Activity Execution

Upon receipt of the message

$$\text{w: START -> ACASE}$$

ACASE transmits concurrently START messages to all activities in the selected list (if it is not empty). When all DONE messages are returned, or if the list is empty, a DONE message is sent by ACASE to its caller. If at least one ERROR message is returned, an ERROR message is issued instead. Then all workers hired during parameter evaluation are fired.

A CASE statement written without an ELSE clause is equivalent to a CASE statement with an ELSE clause followed by an empty lan + 1 list.

15.3.7. Translation of a Segment Definition into the Model

Objects and evaluation tasks with associated workers of sections 15.3.1 to 15.3.6 preexist to any segment written in pscl. Defining a new segment in pscl corresponds in the model to creating an evaluation task and workers to execute it in the case of a description or operation segment, and to adding new objects and operations in the case of a type, class or language segment. In the following, we shall continue to assume that all expressions and activity invocations written in the body of a segment definition are transformed to standard prefix notation prior to any translation into the worker model.

15.3.7.1. Translation of a CONLAN Segment

A CONLAN segment defines a new Language. It is a list of TYPE, CLASS, DESCRIPTION, FUNCTION and ACTIVITY segments. Translating a CONLAN segment amounts to building a new universe of objects and establishing the pre-defined tasks available to the users of the new language.

15.3.7.2. Translation of a CLASS Segment

A CLASS segment definition serves to group together types, with the objective of static verification of attribute parameters. The translation of a CLASS segment "c" into the model creates a Boolean function Fc on the model universe, called the characteristic function of CLASS c:

$Fc(x) = \underline{true}$ if x is the fully qualified designator of a member of c

$Fc(x) = \underline{false}$ otherwise.

15.3.7.3. Translation of a TYPE Segment

A TYPE segment definition has the effect of enlarging the model universe, and adding new tasks to the set of available evaluation tasks. The following actions take place:

- If the TYPE segment is not derived from cell@, i.e., is not a member of CLASS carr_type, the model universe is augmented with the denotations of all elements of the type. If the TYPE segment is derived from cell@, the model universe is augmented with the names of all the cell workers that may be hired when elements of the type must be obtained. It is assumed that there exist a uniform mechanism for naming cell workers: a free identifier is prefixed with the fully qualified type designator. In the following, however, shorter notations will be used when there is no ambiguity.

- The fully qualified designator of the new TYPE segment is added to the model universe.

- The membership of the new type to all existing classes, and the value of all characteristic functions Fc applied to the new type designator are established.

- An evaluation task is created for every operation carried to, or defined in the TYPE segment. This task is identified by the operation name prefixed with the fully qualified type designator.

If the Type segment is parameterized all the above actions are (conceptually) done for all possible actual attributes.

15.3.7.4. Processing ATT Parameters of a FUNCTION, ACTIVITY or DESCRIPTION Segment

Segment attributes of an operation or DESCRIPTION segment definition are translated in the model to parameters of evaluation tasks. When the segment is referenced in a CONLAN text, attributes must be statically known, else an error is detected. Actual attributes are made part of the segment designator, and are provided to the recruiter when a worker is hired for the task.

Thus, during the dynamic evaluation of a CONLAN text, actual attributes appear as second level parameters of SEND messages addressed to the recruiter. Once a worker has been received for the parameterized task, COMPUTE or EVAL messages to this worker contain no attribute parameters.

15.3.7.5. Translation of an ACTIVITY or FUNCTION Segment

An ACTIVITY (FUNCTION) segment definition is translated into an ACTIVITY (FUNCTION) evaluation task, as defined in section 15.2.3 This task may be divided into 3 main phases.

Initialization

If the operation is defined as STATIC, the initialization phase contains message to the recruiter to hire

- a cell worker for each locally declared carrier

- an operation worker for each occurrence of STATIC operation invocation

Parameter Evaluation phase

An EVAL (COMPUTE) message skeleton is generated, which will be used by an ACTIVITY (FUNCTION) worker who evaluates the task to accept or reject a received EVAL (COMPUTE) message. The EVAL (or COMPUTE) message skeleton holds one parameter for each non-ATT formal parameter of the operation segment, and for each imported object. The position of a parameter in the message skeleton corresponds to the order of the formal parameter or imported object in the pscl text. The type of each parameter is indicated. The actions for the evaluation of actual parameter expressions and type checking of the returned result are generated according to Section 15.2.3.3. This establishes in particular that all actual parameters corresponding to writable formal parameters (keyword W) are carriers and thus belong to a type of class carr_type, i.e., to type cell@ or a type derived from cell@. All cell workers corresponding to actual parameters are made part of the operation team of workers for the duration of the operation evaluation. If an actual parameter corresponds to a formal carrier parameter with W access right, the access right of the actual carrier is expanded by the message:

$$op: id, PERMIT \rightarrow actual$$

An operation gets to know other workers by two distinct mechanisms: hiring them, or getting them as actual parameters. If two activities are invoked with the same actual cell in a W position, and both of them invoke put@ on that cell, the description is nondeterministic at the pscl level.

If assertions are written about the parameters in the operation definition, the evaluation task includes the following actions:

- hire for each asserted boolean expression a worker capable of evaluating it

- send concurrently to all these workers a COMPUTE message with its actual parameters

- test all answered RESULT messages. If at least one contains false, an error is detected.

At the end of the parameter evaluation phase, if an error has been found, an ERROR message is sent back to the invoking worker, and the task evaluation is stopped.

Otherwise:

- in the case of a FUNCTION the next phase follows immediately

- in the case of an ACTIVITY, an EVALUATED message is sent to the invoking worker. Reception of a START message is prescribed before proceeding to the next phase.

BODY Evaluation Phase

Translation of the BODY of an operation segment written in pscl corresponds to specifying the evaluation task as a sequence of groups of concurrent messages to be sent and received. They are the following:

If the operation segment is dynamic, and internal carriers are declared, hire the corresponding cell workers by issueing for each one a SEND message to the recruiter. When all RECEIVE messages are obtained, proceed. If the BODY has a nonempty operation invocation part, then it amounts to a list of put@ invocations, conditional invocations, or user-defined activity invocations. Hire a worker capable of executing each invocation of a non STATIC activity, including conditions, and for each asserted Boolean expression in the body. When all RECEIVE messages are obtained, proceed.

Concurrently send an EVAL message with its actual parameters to each (static or dynamic) ACTIVITY worker and a COMPUTE message to all workers associated with asserted boolean expressions in the body If at least one ERROR message is received or one of the assertions returns false, issue an ERROR message to the invoking worker. Fire all workers hired during this phase and stop.

If all workers return an EVALUATED message, concurrently send to all of them a START message. If at least one ERROR message is returned, issue an ERROR message to the caller with all necessary explanations; fire all workers hired during this phase, and stop.

Otherwise, when all DONE messages have been received, if assertions are written about local carriers in the BODY of the operation segment, hire for each asserted boolean expression a worker to evaluate it; COMPUTE messages are sent concurrently to all these workers. If at least one RESULT message contains false, return an ERROR message to the caller; fire all workers hired during this phase, and stop. If no assertion was written or if all assertions have returned true, the BODY evaluation phase was completed without error.

If the operation is an ACTIVITY segment, this is the end of the task. Fire all workers hired during this phase, send to all carriers corresponding to parameters with W access right FORBID messages and answer a DONE message to the caller.

If the operation is a FUNCTION segment, evaluate the RETURN expression by hiring a worker w capable of computing the outer function of this expression put in prefix notation, and transmitting the message

$$f: COMPUTE(a1,a2,...am) \rightarrow w$$

The obtained answer, whether it is an ERROR or a RESULT message, is propagated by the function to his caller. Fire all workers hired during this phase and stop.

Example of Function Without BODY Part

```
FUNCTION max(x,y: int): int
        RETURN IF x > y THEN x ELSE y ENDIF
ENDmax
```

Invocation of max(59+1, 3*4) results in the following exchange of COMPUTE and RESULT messages.

```
caller: COMPUTE(int.plus(59,1),int.times(3,4)) -> max
"/ parameter evaluation /"
max: COMPUTE(59,1) -> int.plus
max: COMPUTE(3,4) -> int.times
        +
max <- int.plus: RESULT(60)
max <- int.times: RESULT(12)


"/ RETURN expression evaluation /"
max: COMPUTE(int.greater(60,12),60,12) -> IF
        +
IF: COMPUTE(60,12) -> int.greater
        +
IF <- int.greater: RESULT(true)
        +
max <- IF: RESULT(60)
        +
caller <- max: RESULT(60)
```

Example of Function with a BODY Part

```
FUNCTION xor(x,y: bool): bool
 BODY
   DECLARE a: cell@(bool) END
   IF x=0 & y=0 THEN put@(a,0)
   ELIF x=1 & y=1 THEN put@(a,0)
   ELSE put@(a,1) ENDIF
 RETURN get@(a)
ENDxor
```

Invocation of xor(r1, r2), with r1 and r2 being <u>true</u> results in the following exchange of messages.

```
caller: COMPUTE(r1, r2) -> xor
"/ obtain local carriers and workers /"
xor: SEND(cell@(bool)) -> recruiter
xor: SEND(AIF) -> recruiter
       +
xor <- recruiter: RECEIVE(a)
xor <- recruiter: RECEIVE(AIF_1)


"/ body evaluation /"
xor: caller, EVAL(bool.and(bool.equal(true,false),
         bool.equal(true,false)),put@(a,false),
      IF(bool.and(bool.equal(true,true),bool.equal(true,true)),
       put@(a,false),put@(a,true))) -> AIF_1
       +
   ........


AIF_1: COMPUTE(bool.equal(true,false),
         bool.equal(true,false)) -> bool.and_1
       +
   .....


       +
AIF_1 <- bool.and_1: RESULT(false)
       +
AIF_1: caller, EVAL(bool.and(bool.equal(true,true),
         bool.equal(true,true)),
       put@(a,false),put@(a,true)) -> AIF_2
       +
   .......
```

AIF_2: COMPUTE(bool.equal(<u>true</u>,<u>true</u>),
    bool.equal(<u>true</u>,<u>true</u>)) -> bool.and_2
  +
  .....

  +
AIF_2 <- bool.and_2: RESULT(<u>true</u>)
  +
AIF_2: caller, EVAL(a,<u>false</u>) -> put@
  +
AIF_2 <- put@: EVALUATED
  +
AIF_1 <- AIF_2: EVALUATED
  +
xor <- AIF_1: EVALUATED
  +
xor: START -> AIF_1
  +
AIF_1: START -> AIF_2
  +
AIF_2: START -> put@
  +
put@: PUT(<u>false</u>) -> a
  +
put@ <- a: DONE
  +
AIF_2 <- put@: DONE
  +
AIF_1 <- AIF_2: DONE
  +
xor <- AIF_1: DONE

"/ RETURN expression evaluation /"
xor: COMPUTE(a) -> get@
  +
get@: GET -> a
  +
get@ <- a: RESULT(<u>false</u>)
  +
xor <- get@: RESULT(<u>false</u>)
  +
caller <- xor: RESULT(<u>false</u>)

Remarks

The evaluation model for primitive and user defined operations in pscl has a number of implications .

a) Carriers local to an operation, accessed through their attached cell worker, are only known locally.

b) The evaluation model ensures that the lexical order in which activity invocations are written in a segment BODY has no influence on the contents stored in the carriers. Old contents of carriers are retrieved during parameter evaluation. New contents are stored during the activity execution stage.

c) If two invocations of an activity are directed to the same carrier during the second stage, the worker attached to that cell receives two PUT messages. These messages are taken one after the other in an order that cannot be determined from the outside, and the final content of the cell is not predictable. This nondeterministic behavior is not considered to be an error in pscl. Errors due to multiple, simultaneous invocations of an activity will be introduced with the definition of carriers in bcl.

d) Workers attached to dynamic operations (functions and activities) are hired and dismissed for each invocation. Moreover, each dynamic operation invocation amounts to hiring a new set of workers attached to new internal carriers and internal operation invocations for the duration of the evaluation; the whole team is thrown out after all invocations in the BODY have been evaluated (in the case of an activity segment), or after the RETURN expression has been evaluated (in the case of a function segment). This implies that dynamic operations have no memory in the sense that the result of every invocation is independent of the previous invocations.

e) Conversely, workers attached to static operations, and their sub-teams attached to internal cells and internal static operation invocations, are hired once and for all, during the initialization phase of the invoking operation or decription segment. This guarantees that static operations have memory, in the sense that internal cells have, at the beginning of each invocation, their content at the end of the previous invocation.

15.3.7.6. Translation of a Description Segment

A DESCRIPTION segment models a digital system with fixed structure: all the carriers and instances of descriptions that are part of it are statically defined. CONLAN does not provide any facility for dynamic creation/destruction of modules. Each instance of description only has access to its interface carriers, to its local carriers, and to the interface carriers of immediately embodied instances of description; all of these carriers are associated with the instance at compile time, and are permanent during the evaluation. However, the environment, and the hardware designer through it, has extended rights: he can access all the carriers known by any instance, at any level of nesting.

A description may be decomposed into smaller descriptions to reflect the anticipated physical structure of a system. Decomposition is also a well recognized design technique; however, choosing one decomposition, or another, or none at all should have no influence on the result of a simulation run, provided the hardware described is the same and the description is deterministic. The model of evaluation of nested instances of DESCRIPTION segments at the pscl level, and in a later paragraph the evaluation at the bcl level, fulfills this requirement.

A DESCRIPTION segment is translated into a DESCRIPTION evaluation task, as defined in section 15.2.4. All the rules for hiring interface elements, and adjusting their capabilities to take IN, OUT and INOUT directions into account are those of paragraph 15.2.4.1. If the description BODY has a non-empty operation invocation part, its translation into hiring/firing actions, EVAL + EVALUATED and START +

DONE message exchanges, and the production of the EVAL message parameters are identical to what is being done for ACTIVITY segments except for the fact that the DESCRIPTION segment worker gives his own name as context of SEND and EVAL messages. Assertions are also processed in the same way: those written before the BODY are evaluated during the EVAL + EVALUATED phase, those written in the BODY are evaluated at the end of the START + DONE phase. In addition, if the DESCRIPTION segment contains nested instances, EVAL + EVALUATED and START + DONE messages are to be exchanged with each instance, concurrently with the messages exchanged with activity workers.

It should be noted that instances of descriptions, aside from fixing their context, act as mere transmitters of messages between their enclosing segment, and their own local activity invocations and enclosed instances. Therefore, structuring finely a description into many levels of nested segments adds layers of message passing, but has no influence on the result of evaluation.

Example: Nested descriptions are provided by:

```
DESCRIPTION x1(IN start: cell@(bool))
BODY
   DESCRIPTION inside(IN a: cell@(int), OUT b: cell@(int))
   BODY
   IF empty@(a) THEN put@(b,0)
           ELSE put@(b,get@(a)+1) ENDIF
   ENDinside
DECLARE x, y, z: cell@(int) ENDDECLARE
USE inner: inside ENDUSE
put@(inner.a, get@(x)),
put@(x, min(2*get@(x),8)),
put@(y, get@(inner.b)),
IF get@(start) THEN put@(z, get@(z)+get@(y)) ENDIF
ENDx1
```

In the following, let x1 designate a worker who evaluates the task associated with the above DESCRIPTION segment x1; similarly, all worker names of the team are very close to the identifiers in the pscl text, as an aid to the reader. Assuming that x1 is the outer segment being evaluated, the initialization of x1 and the reception by inner of its interface cells are done by the following exchange of messages:

```
"/ reception of the interface cell /"
environment: RECEIVE(start) -> x1
   +

"/ hiring the nested instance of description /"
x1: SEND(inside) -> recruiter
   +
x1 <- recruiter:RECEIVE(inner)
   +
```

"/ hiring local cells /"
x1: SEND(cell@(int)) -> recruiter
  +
x1 <- recruiter:RECEIVE(a)
  +
x1: SEND(cell@(int)) -> recruiter
  +
x1 <- recruiter:RECEIVE(b)
  +
x1: SEND(cell@(int)) -> recruiter
  +
x1 <- recruiter:RECEIVE(x)
  +
x1: SEND(cell@(int)) -> recruiter
  +
x1 <- recruiter:RECEIVE(y)
  +
x1: SEND(cell@(int)) -> recruiter
  +
x1 <- recruiter:RECEIVE(z)
  +

"/ removing x1 from the capability of b /"
x1: FORBID -> b
  +
x1 <- b:DONE
  +

"/ sending his interface to inner /"
x1: RECEIVE(a) -> inner
x1: RECEIVE(b) -> inner ·

"/ add inner to the capability of b /"
inner: inner,PERMIT -> b
  +
inner <- b: DONE

One full evaluation of x1 would produce the following pattern of message exchanges:

environment: environment,EVAL -> x1
  +

"/ hiring workers for dynamic activity invocations /"
x1: SEND(cell@(int).put@) -> recruiter
  +

x1 <- recruiter:RECEIVE(put@1)
  +

x1: SEND(cell@(int).put@) -> recruiter
  +

x1 <- recruiter:RECEIVE(put@2)
  +

x1: SEND(cell@(int).put@) -> recruiter
  +

x1 <- recruiter:RECEIVE(put@3)
  +

x1: SEND(AIF) -> recruiter
  +

x1 <- recruiter:RECEIVE(AIF1)
  +

"/ broadcasting EVAL messages to internal segments /"
x1: x1,EVAL(a, get@(x)) -> put@1
x1: x1,EVAL(x, min(int.times($\underline{2}$,get@(x)),$\underline{8}$) -> put@2
x1: x1,EVAL(y, get@(b)) -> put@3
x1: x1,EVAL(get@(start), put@(z, int.plus(get@(z), get@(y))),()) -> AIF1
x1: x1,EVAL -> inner
  +

```
"/ parameter evaluation stage for the internal segments /"
inner: SEND(AIF) -> recruiter
   +
inner <- recruiter: RECEIVE(AIF2)
   +
inner: inner,EVAL(empty@(a),put@(b,0),
            put@(b,int.plus(get@(a),1))) -> AIF2
   +
AIF2: SEND(empty@) -> recruiter
   +
AIF2 <- recruiter: RECEIVE(empty@1)
   +
AIF2: COMPUTE(a) -> empty@1
   +
AIF2 <- empty@: RESULT(false)
   +
AIF2: SEND(put@) -> recruiter
   +
AIF2 <- recruiter: RECEIVE(put@4)
   +
AIF2: inner,EVAL(b,0) -> put@4
   +


"/ reception of EVALUATED messages /"
AIF2 <- put@4: EVALUATED
inner <- AIF2: EVALUATED
x1 <- inner: EVALUATED
x1 <- AIF1: EVALUATED
x1 <- put@1: EVALUATED
x1 <- put@2: EVALUATED
x1 <- put@3:EVALUATED
   +
environment <- x1: EVALUATED
   +


"/ START + DONE phase /"
environment: environment, START -> x1
   +
x1: START -> put@1
   ....
```

```
x1: START -> inner
   +
x1 <- put@1:DONE
x1 <- put@2:DONE
   ....

x1 <- inner:DONE
   +
environment <- x1:DONE
```

16. An Example of Type Derivation in Pscl

TYPE tern BODY   "/Type name is tern/"
  { 0, 1, 'U' }   "/Enumerated Set (elements taken from univ@)/"
  CARRY equal, notequal ENDCARRY   "/Operations carried from the
                                             base type (univ@)/"

FUNCTION leq(x, y: tern): bool   "/Operation Definition"/
  RETURN IF $(x = 0) \mid (y = 1)$ THEN 1   "/Use of carried operations/"
    ELIF $(x = \text{'U'}) \& (y = \text{'U'})$ THEN 1
    ELSE 0 ENDIF
  FORMAT@   "/grammmar extension/"
    EXTEND expression_4.05   "/index into grammar (alternative name)/"
    MEANS leq(@1, @2) ENDFORMAT   "/extend meaning of =</"
ENDleq

FUNCTION lt(x, y: tern): bool
  RETURN $(x =< y) \& \sim(x = y)$ "/Use leq via syntax defined above/"
  FORMAT@ EXTEND expression_4.04
       MEANS lt(@1,@2) ENDFORMAT   "/extend </"
ENDlt

FUNCTION gt(x, y: tern): bool
  RETURN $\sim(x =< y)$
  FORMAT@ EXTEND expression_4.07
       MEANS gt(@1,@2) ENDFORMAT   "/extend >/"
ENDgt

FUNCTION geq(x, y: tern): bool
  RETURN $\sim(x < y)$
  FORMAT@ EXTEND expression_4.06
```
```

```
            MEANS geq(@1,@2) ENDFORMAT                        "/extend >=/"
ENDgeq

FUNCTION and(x, y: tern): tern
   RETURN IF (x = 0) | (y = 0) THEN 0
      ELIF (x = 1) & (y = 1) THEN 1
      ELSE 'U' ENDIF
   FORMAT@ EXTEND expression_3.02
            MEANS and(@1,@2) ENDFORMAT                        "/extend  &/"
ENDand

FUNCTION or(x, y: tern): tern
   RETURN IF (x = 1) | (y = 1) THEN 1
      ELIF (x = 0) & (y = 0) THEN 0
      ELSE 'U' ENDIF
   FORMAT@ EXTEND expression_1.02
            MEANS or(@1,@2) ENDFORMAT                         "/extend |/"
ENDor

FUNCTION not(x :tern): tern
   RETURN IF x = 1 THEN 0 ELIF x = 0 THEN 1 ELSE 'U' ENDIF
   FORMAT@ EXTEND expression_8.02
            MEANS not(@1) ENDFORMAT                           "/extend  ~/"
ENDnot

FUNCTION nand(x, y: tern): tern
   RETURN ~(x & y)
   FORMAT@ EXTEND expression_3.03
            MEANS nand(@1,@2) ENDFORMAT                       "/extend ~&/"
ENDnand

FUNCTION nor(x, y: tern): tern
   RETURN ~(x | y)
   FORMAT@ EXTEND expression_1.03
            MEANS nor(@1,@2) ENDFORMAT                        "/extend ~|/"
ENDnor
ENDtern
```

IV Base CONLAN

17. Introduction

In this part a new member of the CONLAN family called Base CONLAN (in short: bcl) is defined. It is designed to serve as a root language for CONLAN toolmakers from which all further members of the CONLAN family are to be derived. This part of the report formally defines and documents bcl.

The CONLAN construct used to define new languages is the **language definition segment** which has been introduced in Section 2.4 and 10.7. Each new language presumes the existence of an existing, older language which is used as a base or reference, providing an initial syntax and semantics defined by a grammar, a set of types, classes and operations as well as an associated model of computation. This syntax and semantics can then be extended or reduced in the new language. In this regard, bcl is not different from any other member of the CONLAN family. We define it by building its types, classes and operations from pscl as the reference language using the CONLAN construction mechanism, syntax and semantics described in part II.

The objects and operations of pscl have been chosen primarily with mathematical generality and simplicity in mind. Most of them have therefore no direct relation to hardware description.

The purpose of bcl is (i) to add to the object types of pscl new object types and freestanding operations, which reflect the specific CONLAN concept of hardware description in time and space, (ii) to extend the pscl syntax to incorporate convenient denotations for these objects and operations via appropriate FORMAT statements, (iii) to extend the pscl model of computation to support the bcl model of time (Section 17.2).

17.1. Bcl Object Types and Operations

17.1.1. Basic Categories

With respect to the points of definition and possible points of reference of types and operations, i.e. their visibility, the following three categories can be associated with bcl as well as with any other language of the CONLAN family derived from bcl:

1. Bcl defined toolmaker types and operations are defined in the CONLAN bcl segment in Section 18 with fully qualified names containing at least one identifier terminating with symbol '@'. They may only be used for the derivation of a new language from bcl, i.e. be referenced only within the scope of the CONLAN bcl segment itself or a CONLAN segment having bcl as its reference language.

2. Bcl defined user types and operations are defined in the CONLAN segment defining bcl with fully qualified names containing no identifier terminated by symbol '@'. Besides their use in language derivation, they may also be used for writing descriptions or operations i.e. be referenced in freestanding DESCRIPTION, ACTIVITY or FUNCTION segments for which bcl is the reference language.

3. User defined types and operations written in bcl are defined in freestanding DESCRIPTION,

ACTIVITY or FUNCTION segments with bcl as the reference language by derivation from some bcl defined user type with names containing no identifier terminating with symbol "@". They may only be referenced within the scope of the segment in which they are defined (see Section 9.3.2).

With respect to representation and operative properties, the types associated with bcl may be subdivided in three categories:

- scalar data types

- constructors for arrays and records

- toolmaker types

These three categories are discussed in the following sections.

17.1.2. Scalar Data Types

As indicated in Section 4.1, three classes of scalar data types are distinguished in bcl:

value types   whose elements are static objects that do not change with time.

signal types   whose elements are sequences of values over time.

carrier types   whose elements are cells containing signals, i.e. signal carriers.

Each class is formally defined in Section 18 via a CLASS segment to comprise

- a number of basic bcl defined types and type families,

- all user defined types which may be derived from them.

Identifiers "val_type", "sig_type" and "carr_type" are introduced along with their formal definition as designator for the three classes. They serve as a formal definition and unambiguous base for type checking and invocation of parameter matching functions.

17.1.2.1. CLASS val_type

The bcl defined user types for class "val_type" are types "int", "bool" and "string", known from pscl, plus three subtypes of "int", namely positive integers "pint", non-negative integers "nnint" and a family of bounded integers "bint(m,n: int)". There are no bcl defined toolmaker types included in this class.

17.1.2.2. CLASS sig_type

For this class bcl defines a basic user type family

TYPE signal(x: val_type)

It designates all possible mappings of elements of a given value type x onto the bcl model of time (Section

17.2 and 17.3). The properties of this type family are outlined in Section 4.5 and are formally defined in Section 18.13. It provides a delay function, allowing its user to look up past values of a signal. In addition two INTERPRETER@ functions "val" and "pack" are provided which are automatically invoked by the environment, whenever required for type matching (Section 17.3.3) during parameter evaluation.

17.1.2.3. CLASS carr_type
For this class, bcl contributes three basic carrier type families

1. TYPE terminal(x: val_type; def: x) with user activity **connect**

2. TYPE variable(x: val_type; def: x) with user activity **assign**

3. TYPE rtvariable(x: val_type; def: x) with user activity **transfer**

Carrier types from the three families designate cells holding signals on scalar values. They differ with respect to the retention properties of their elements at the computation step and time interval (see bcl model of time Section 17.2).

Parameter def denotes a default value to be used during initialization and when no user activity is invoked.

The properties of the three carrier type families have been outlined in Section 4.6 and are formally developed in Section 18.15. The formal development covers, in addition to the user activities, a number of INTERPRETER@ functions and activities which are automatically invoked by the bcl-environment (Section 17.3) to cover type matching (functions "val", "sig", "pack") and signal updating (activities "finstep", "finint", "shrink" and "setlength") .

17.1.3. Constructor Types for Arrays and Records
Bcl provides a number of types and generic type families for toolmakers to support the definition of spatially stuctured object types for languages derived from bcl.

Generic TYPE **array@(u: any@)** (Section 18.9) represents the CONLAN concept of arrays. It comprises all arrays of objects of a given type u with an arbitrary number of dimensions, and with arbitrary left_bound and right_bound indices in each dimension together with a sizable number of operations.

A number of user functions are associated with TYPE array@ to sense the number and left- and right-bounds of dimensions, to compare, transpose and catenate arrays, to select elements and slices from arrays. The selecting functions are supported by TYPE **indexer@** (Section 18.8) to provide a convenient constant denotation for the specification of single or multiple indices and index ranges at the point reference to an array. The identifiers for all functions specified on TYPE indexer@ are terminated by "@" and thus only available to the toolmaker to specify selection processes in arrays.

In addition, a number of toolmaker operations are specified on arrays. Some serve as auxiliary functions for the specification of user functions. Other generic operations can be used to transport conveniently elementary operations on the element type u of the array to arrays of this type as a whole by the combination of corresponding array elements (e.g. redefine "add" known on integers for arrays of integers).

SUBTYPE **fixed_array@(u: any@; d: array_dimension@)** (Section 18.10) designates the subset of all arrays on elements of type u with a fixed number of dimensions and a fixed left- and right-bound in each of these dimensions specified by parameter d. For this purpose a supporting TYPE **array_dimension@** (Section 18.7) is supplied to provide a convenient constant denotation for parameter d at the point of declaration. Operations on type array_dimension are made available only to the toolmaker by terminating their identifiers with symbol "@". They are used within the definition of the operations on arrays in Section 18.9.

TYPE **record@(f: field_descriptor_list@)** (Section 18.11) represents the CONLAN record concept. It permits the toolmaker to define types of structured objects whose elements are of different but predefined type, as in many programming languages. Supporting TYPE **field_descriptor@** (Section 18.11) provides a convenient denotation to specify the name and type of each field in the record at the point of declaration. All functions on this type are for toolmakers only. A user FUNCTION **record_select** is associated with TYPE record to allow the selection of a specific field from a record at the point of reference with a convenient notation (infix symbol '!').

17.1.4. Toolmaker Types

In addition to the constructor types for arrays and records described in the preceeding section a number of additional toolmaker types are found in the formal development of bcl in Section 18. They are introduced mainly as auxiliary types to simplify the construction of user types. Typical examples are **tytuple@(t: any@)**, **range@**, **cs_signal@(t: any@)**.

Other toolmaker types are intended specifically for the derivation of other user languages from bcl. Typical are the generalized generic carrier type families **terminal@**, **variable@** and **rtvariable@** and the generalized "**signal@**" serving as father type families for the corresponding user type families discussed above.

TYPE terminal@(x: any@, def: x; cd: bool) for example is not restricted to carry signals of scalar values. It can be used to derive e.g. a terminal type carrying signals on vectors of values. In addition, parameter cd allows a toolmaker to disable the normal collision handling mechanism used for activity "connect" in the user version, which provides an error message if two or more simultaneous invocations of "connect" on the same terminal attempt to set its signal to different values. Thus types of terminals can be derived for other languages update signals with values such as 'u' to denote undefined.

17.1.5. User Types

The user types of bcl which may be referenced in descriptions are all those types which are contained in CLASS val_type, sig_type and carr_type (Section 17.1.2). Therefore, from the point of view of the user, bcl is essentially a scalar language.

The complete derivation tree for the bcl types is shown in Figure 17-1. Toolmaker types are marked by circles, user types by squares.

17.2. CONLAN Model of Time

CONLAN arrays and records are similar to those of programming languages and we expect the readers to have little difficulty following the development of these types in Section 18.8, 18.9 and 18.10 after the introduction given in Section 17.1.3. Signals and carriers on the other hand, as defined in Section 18.13 and 18.15 for bcl, are specific CONLAN concepts, which are intended as a base for the definition of the signal and carrier types of all further languages derived from bcl. Therefore we feel it necessary to provide some more informal information of the extensions to the pscl evaluation mechanism and the concept of time used in

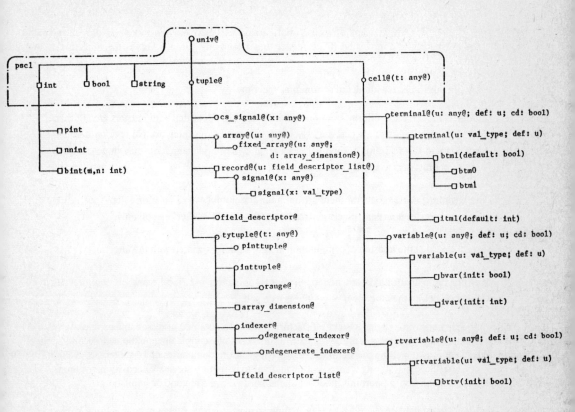

○ Bcl-Defined Toolmaker Types

□ Bcl-Defined User Types

Figure 17-1: bcl derivation Tree

CONLAN. The CONLAN concept of signals and carriers is based on our model of time thus, their development will be better appreciated if the reader understands the latter. This is the objective of this section.

CONLAN provides a discrete model of continuous, real time.

1. Real time is broken into uniform durations called "intervals" identified with integers greater than zero. Ascending, successive integers are associated with contiguous intervals. No relation between the interval and the real time second exists in general. An implementation may impose such a relation or permit users to specify such a relation.

2. At the beginning of each interval there are an indefinite number of calculation "steps" identified with integers greater than zero. Successive steps provide a before/after relation only.

3. Values obtained at the last step of computation are the values associated with the interval.

4. When operation invocations are nested, the inner operation use 'local steps' to complete its computation before the outer operation utilizes its result.

When modeling a specific digital system satisfactory results are obtained at reasonable computational cost by quantizing time to some fraction of the second; for purposes of example assume the nanosecond. Actual binary signals are constrained by this quantization to change at the boundaries of 1 ns intervals. Computing the value of a specific signal during a specific 1 ns interval may require successive activity invocations. The CONLAN interval and step support this model of digital hardware and method of simulation.

No real time is thought to elapse when evaluating a mathematical function or executing a computer program. Yet many successive computational steps are usually required. Again the CONLAN model of time supports such computation by distinquishing steps within an interval. While stepping through an interval, its identifying integer does not advance.

17.3. System Interfaces
System interfaces are facilities provided to toolmakers to interact with the environment. They are used to interrogate the environment or to supplement it by providing default actions to be taken in the absence of appropriate step or interval computations.

17.3.1. Activity error@
This primitive activity is automatically invoked by the environment whenever an ASSERT expression yields '0' or types of formal and actual parameters do not match or belong to non-matching classes (see Section 17.3.3). Subsequent actions are determined by the sophistication of the environment. All processing might stop, or if the nature of the error is determined, a default value may be returned and processing continued timidly.

17.3.2. Real Time Counter t@

t@ is an object of type cell@(int) whose value is the current time interval. Contiguous values are provided in ascending order starting with one.

17.3.3. Parameter matching functions

Parameter matching functions are specified with signal types (CLASS sig_type) and carrier types (CLASS carr_type) prefixing the definition with keyword INTERPRETER@. Invocations of these functions are automatically inserted into the actual parameter lists at compile time at positions where the actual parameter type does not match the formal parameter type. Thus they need not be explicitly stated by the user. Identifiers "val", "sig" and "pack" denote them.

val
This function may be applied either to a signal or a carrier. It returns the last value of the actual signal or of the signal contained in the actual carrier. Function "val" must be defined explicitly for each type of CLASS sig_type or CLASS carr_type.

sig
Function "sig" may be applied to carriers only. It extracts the signal from this carrier. Function "sig" must be defined explicitly for each type of CLASS carr_type.

pack
Function "pack" may be applied to a value only. It returns a signal containing this value in all step positions of all intervals. Function "pack" must be defined explicitly for each type of CLASS sig_type.

Invocation of parameter matching is governed by the classes to which corresponding actual and formal parameters belong. The parameter matching table for bcl is shown in Table 17-1.

parameter class		INTERPRETER@
formal	actual	FUNCTION
val_type	sig_type	val
val_type	carr_type	val
sig_type	val_type	pack
sig_type	carr_type	sig
carr_type	val_type	-[4]
carr_type	sig_type	-

Table 17-1: Bcl parameter matching table

17.3.4. Signal Modification Activities in Carriers

Signal modification activities may be defined for carrier types which are invoked by the environment. Their definition must be prefixed with keyword INTERPRETER@. For each bcl carrier type four activities of this kind are defined and denoted by reserved identifiers "finstep", "finint", "shrink" and "setlength".

---

[4]Illegal combinations generate an error message at compile time

finstep   Activity "finstep" is applied to each carrier by its environment at the end of each computation step. It extends the signal of each carrier by some prescribed value if its signal has not been extended by the evaluation of some explicit activity invocation during this step. The value appended depends on the particular carrier type.

finint   Activity "finint" is applied to a carrier by its environment to extend its signal by one time interval with a first value in this interval, after the last computation step of the current time interval t@ has been executed. The last computation step is determined by stabilisation of all carriers within the scope of one segment (Section 9.3.2). The value appended depends on the particular carrier type.

shrink   Activity "shrink" is applied to each carrier by its environment at the end of each computation step after the stabilisation test. It eliminates from the signal contained in this carrier the old value of the previous step and establishes the new value as the current step value.

setlength   Activity "setlength" is applied to a local carrier of a static function or activity before each evaluation of the body. It adjusts the length of a signal held in that carrier which can be different to the current signal length through the effect of conditional invocation.

17.4. CONLAN Model of Signal Computation

Hardware descriptions record how the signal parts of some carriers are related to those of carriers with known signal parts such as constants in a manner that displays behavior and/or structure and supports computation of those unknown signal parts. Such computation is usually performed viewing past and present signal values as "known" and future values as "unknown." With each computational step, known values are used by the invoked activities on these carriers to determine a future value and thereby change its status to known.

CONLAN signals gain a new value with each calculation step and real time interval. Activity finstep provides default signal growth for a step in which no user invoked activity extends a signal. Activity finint is invoked if all carriers have been stabilized and provides the first value for the next real time interval. These activities are invoked automatically by the environment, and not by CONLAN users or toolmakers.

A global step counter s@ is maintained by the environment for the outermost description segment and for all instances of descriptions nested in it. It is incremented for each computation step during evaluation of this segment structure. When the environment determines that all signals have attained stable values, it increments the value provided by t@ and resets the s@ counter to 1. It detects calculation step oscillation (s@ reaches a predetermined limit) and responds to it with a message and optionally termination of document evaluation or continuation using the signal values available at the last step of calculation. In addition a local step counter is created by the environment for each (dynamic) invocation of an operation to monitor proper termination of the evaluation of this operation at the step level.

Figure 17-2(a) shows an example of the value part of a 3 time interval boolean signal with t@ = 3 being the current interval. Each time interval comprises a computation step signal with a varying number of computation steps depending on the number of steps needed to attain stability. Signals in carriers are kept in a condensed form which contains only the last value in the computation step signal of each time interval except the current which contains the last two values to support the test of stability, as shown in Figure 17-2(b). The model of computation built into the environment creates this form of a signal by invoking activity "shrink" (Section 17.3.4) every time a new time interval or calculation step is begun. Figure 17-2(c) shows the same signal after applying "shrink".

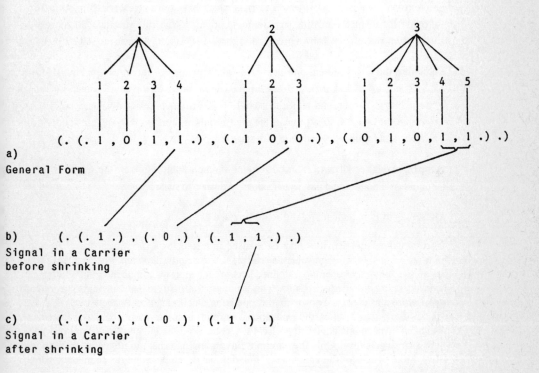

Figure 17-2: Examples of 3 time unit CONLAN boolean signal

Base CONLAN (bcl) is constructed in Chapter 18 from pscl so as to support this model of computation for all further languages. A step of signal computation at the base level of descriptive abstraction corresponds to a computation step and consists of the following stages:

Stage	Description
1	For each invoked activity and function of the system description under evaluation,

Stage	Description
1	For each invoked activity and function of the system description under evaluation, determine via the description of that invoked module the value part(s) of carriers for the next step from known present and past signal values. ·Advance to stage 2.
2	Determine via **finstep** activities on carriers which have not been serviced in stage 1 and provide for them the missing step value according to the rule specified in the activity, future step values from known present and past signal values. Advance to stage 3.
3	Examine the set of present and next step values. If one or more carriers have differing values and s@ is less than a predetermined limit, advance the step counter s@, apply "shrink" to all carriers and return to stage 1. If all carriers have equal values (stabilization) continue with stage 4. If s@ equals the predetermined limit, publish an "oscillation" error message and (optionally) continue with stage 4.
4	Apply "shrink" to all carriers and determine via their **finint** activities future interval values from known present and past signal values. Advance to stage 5.
5	Reset s@ to 1, increment t@, and return to stage 1.

None, one or more functions and activities may be invoked in a step for a specific carrier. If multiple invocations attempt to set a signal to different values, a "collision" exists and will be reported as an error. The primitive operations of pscl and the bcl operations defined later in the report determine the value part (stage 1 above) without the need to store intermediate results. This is not generally true and an operation may require more than one step before the carriers known to the operation stabilize (stage 3 above). When such operations are invoked in a nested fashion, the evaluation algorithm becomes more complex. In essence, stages 1-3 are applied to an invoked operation using a local step counter before the invoking operation utilizes the result in one of its step calculations. Only the outermost invocation in a chain of nested invocations uses s@ as its step counter. More details for this case may be found in the development of the complete model of computation in Chapter 19.

18. Formal Construction of Bcl

18.1. Reference Language

REFLAN pscl   "/All pscl definitions are available
                                                      in the definition of bcl/"

CONLAN bcl
BODY
CARRYALL   "/All pscl definitions are available
                                                      to the user of bcl/"

18.2. Subsets and Ranges of Integers

SUBTYPE nnint BODY   "/nonnegative integers/"
  ALL a: int WITH a $>= 0$ ENDALL
ENDnnint

SUBTYPE pint BODY   "/positive integers/"
  ALL a: int WITH a > 0 ENDALL
ENDpint

SUBTYPE bint(m,n: int) BODY   "/bounded integers/"
  ALL a: int WITH
    IF m $=< n$ THEN (m $=< a$) & (a $=< n$)
        ELSE (n $=< a$) & (a $=< m$)
    ENDIF
  ENDALL
ENDbint   "/e.g. bint(3,-1)={3,2,1,0,-1}/"

18.3. Additional Boolean Operations

FUNCTION nor(x,y: bool): bool
  RETURN ~(x | y)
  FORMAT@   "/Define x~|y to invoke nor(x,y)/"
    EXTEND expression_1.03 E = R expression_1 '~|' expression_2
    MEANS nor(@1,@2)
  ENDFORMAT
ENDnor

FUNCTION xor(x,y: bool): bool   "/eXclusive OR/"
  RETURN x ~= y
  FORMAT@   "/Define x XOR y to invoke xor(x,y)/"
    EXTEND expression_2.02 ER = R expression_2 'XOR' expression_3
    MEANS xor(@1,@2)
  ENDFORMAT
ENDxor

```
FUNCTION eqv(x,y: bool): bool                                    "/EQuiValence/"
  RETURN x = y
  FORMAT@                                    "/Define x EQV y to invoke eqv(x,y)/"
    EXTEND expression_2.03 ER = R expression_2 'EQV' expression_3
    MEANS eqv(@1,@2)
  ENDFORMAT
ENDeqv


FUNCTION nand(x,y: bool): bool
  RETURN ~(x & y)
  FORMAT@                                   "/Define x~&y to invoke nand(x,y)/"
    EXTEND expression_3.03 ER = R expression_3 '~&' expression_4
    MEANS nand(@1,@2)
  ENDFORMAT
ENDnand

FORMAT@                                "/Define x AND y for sequential &/"
                                       "/y is only evaluated if x evaluates to 1/"
  EXTEND expression_3.04 ER = R expression_3 'AND' expression_4
  MEANS IF @1 THEN @2 ELSE 0 ENDIF
ENDFORMAT

FORMAT@                                 "/Define x OR y for sequential |/"
                                        "/y is only evaluated if x evaluates to 0/"
  EXTEND expression_1.04 E = R expression_1 'OR' expression_2
  MEANS IF @1 THEN 1 ELSE @2 ENDIF
ENDFORMAT
```

18.4. Class of Scalar Value Types

"/Class of all types which are not derived from tuple@
and not from cell@/"

```
CLASS val_type  BODY
  ALL x: any@ WITH
    ~(x <| tuple@) & ~(x <| pscl.carr_type)
  ENDALL
ENDval_type
```

18.5. Typed Tuples

TYPE tytuple@(t: any@)   "/Parameterized with a type/"
  BODY
  ALL a: tuple@ WITH
    FORALL@ i: pint IS i > size@(a) OR select@(a,i) .< t ENDFORALL
  ENDALL

  CARRY equal,notequal,size@,remove@ ENDCARRY

  FUNCTION select@(x: tytuple@(t); i: pint): t
    RETURN convert@(select@(old(x),i),t)
    FORMAT@   "/Define x[.y.] to invoke select@(x,y)/"
      EXTEND expression_10.10 ER = R expression_10 '[.' expression_1 '.]'
      MEANS select@(@1,@2)
    ENDFORMAT
  ENDselect@

  FUNCTION tuplize@(x: t): tytuple@(t)   "/Return a tytuple with one element/"
    RETURN THE@ z: tytuple@(t) WITH size@(z) = 1
           select@(old(z),1) = convert@(x,univ@) ENDTHE
  ENDtuplize@

                                                          "/Return x without the first element/"
  FUNCTION tail@(x: tytuple@(t)): tytuple@(t)
    ASSERT size@(x) > 1 ENDASSERT
    RETURN remove@(x,1)
  ENDtail@

  FUNCTION extend@(x: tytuple@(t); a: t): tytuple@(t)   "/Add an element/"
    RETURN new(extend@(old(x),convert@(a,univ@)))
    FORMAT@   "/Define x # y to invoke extend@(x,y)/"
      EXTEND expression_9.02 ER = R expression_9 '#' expression_10
      MEANS extend@(@1,@2)
    ENDFORMAT
  ENDextend@

```
FUNCTION catenate@(x,y: tytuple@(t)): tytuple@(t)                    "/Catenate two tytuples/"
  RETURN IF size@(y) = 0 THEN x
       ELIF size@(y)=1 THEN extend@(x,y[.1.])
              ELSE catenate@(extend@(x,y[.1.]),tail@(y)) ENDIF
  FORMAT@                                            "/Define x # y to invoke catenate@(x,y)/"
    EXTEND expression_9.02
    MEANS catenate@((@1,@2)
  ENDFORMAT
ENDcatenate@



                                                      "/Swap two elements of a tytuple/"
FUNCTION exchange@(x: tytuple@(t); i,j: pint): tytuple@(t)
  ASSERT i =< size@(x) , j =< size@(x) ENDASSERT
  RETURN
    THE@ y: tytuple@(t) WITH
     size@(y) = size@(x) AND
     FORALL@ k: pint IS
      k > size@(x) OR
      select@(old(y),k) = IF k = i THEN select@(old(x),j)
           ELIF k = j THEN select@(old(x),i)
           ELSE select@(old(x),k) ENDIF
     ENDFORALL
    ENDTHE
ENDexchange@



                                         "/Generic function -- Unary operation on tytuples/"
FUNCTION fmon@(x: tytuple@(t); ATT u: any@;
              ATT f: FUNCTION(t): u): tytuple@(u)
  ASSERT size@(x) > 0 ENDASSERT
  RETURN IF size@(x) = 1 THEN tuplize@(f(x[.1.]))
            ELSE tuplize@(f(x[.1.])) # fmon@(tail@(x),u,f)
       ENDIF
ENDfmon@
ENDtytuple@

SUBTYPE pinttuple@ BODY                          "/non-empty tuples of positive integers/"
  ALL a: tytuple@(pint) WITH size@(a) > 0 ENDALL
ENDpinttuple@
```

SUBTYPE inttuple@ BODY   "/non-empty tuples of integers/"
  ALL a: tytuple@(int) WITH size@(a) > 0 ENDALL
ENDinttuple@

"/Example:

Assume the following tuple of strings and function on a string:

DECLARE x: tytuple@(string) = (.'A','B','C','D'.) ENDDECLARE
FUNCTION checkb(s: string): bool RETURN s = 'B' ENDcheckb

x[.3.] or select@(x,3)   = 'C'
tuplize@('E')   = (.'E'.)
tail@(x)   = (.'B','C','D'.)
x # 'E' or extend@(x,'E') = (.'A','B','C','D','E'.)
x # 2 or extend@(x,2)   type error (x is a tuple of strings and 2 an integer)
x # x or catenate@(x,x)   = (.'A','B','C','D','A','B','C','D'.)
exchange@(x,2,3)   = (.'A','C','B','D'.)
fmon@(x,bool,checkb)   = (.0,1,0,0.)
/"

18.6. Range of Integers

TYPE range@ BODY
  ALL a: inttuple@ WITH
    FORALL@ i: pint IS i > size@(a) OR a[.i.] = a[.1.]+i-1 ENDFORALL |
    FORALL@ i: pint IS i > size@(a) OR a[.i.] = a[.1.]-i+1 ENDFORALL
  ENDALL

  CARRY equal,notequal,size@ ENDCARRY

                                              "/No remove@ or extend@ for ranges/"

  FUNCTION lbound@(x: range@): int   "/Left bound/"
    RETURN old(x)[.1.]
  ENDlbound@

  FUNCTION rbound@(x: range@): int   "/Right bound/"
    RETURN old(x)[.size@(x).]
  ENDrbound@

```
FUNCTION isin@(i: int; x: range@): bool                                    "/Is i in range x ?/"
  RETURN IF i >= lbound@(x) THEN i =< rbound@(x) | i = lbound@(x)
           ELSE i >= rbound@(x) ENDIF
ENDisin@



                                                     "/Are all integers of z in range x ?/"
FUNCTION arein@(z: inttuple@; x: range@): bool
  ASSERT size@(z) > 0 ENDASSERT
  RETURN IF size@(z) = 1 THEN isin@(z[.1.],x)
           ELSE isin@(z[.1.],x) & arein@(tail@(z),x) ENDIF
ENDarein@

FUNCTION position@(i: int; x: range@): pint                      "/Position of i in x/"
  ASSERT isin@(i,x) ENDASSERT
  RETURN IF lbound@(x) =< rbound@(x) THEN i-lbound@(x)+1
           ELSE lbound@(x)-i+1 ENDIF
ENDposition@

FUNCTION normalize@(x: range@): range@                          "/Return a 1-origin range/"
  RETURN THE@ y: range@ WITH lbound@(y) = 1 & rbound@(y) = size@(x) ENDTHE
ENDnormalize@

                                          "/Return a 1-origin range r with rbound@(r)=i/"
FUNCTION ordinal_range@(i: pint): range@
  RETURN THE@ x: range@ WITH lbound@(x) = 1 & rbound@(x) = i ENDTHE
ENDordinal_range@

FORMAT@                                "/Define (:x:y:) as the constant denotation of the range r
             with lbound@(r)=x and rbound@(r)=y/"
  EXTEND range_expr.01 ER = R expression_1:int_constant

  EXTEND expression_range.01 R = range_expr ':' range_expr
  MEANS THE@ r: range@ WITH lbound@(r) = @1 & rbound@(r) = @2 ENDTHE

  EXTEND range_denotation.01 R = '(:' expression_range ':)'
  MEANS (@1)

  EXTEND unsigned_constant_denotation.06 E = R range_denotation
ENDFORMAT                                      "/i.e. (:3:5:) stands for the range (.3,4,5.)/"
ENDrange@
```

"/Example:

Assume the following declarations:

DECLARE
  x: range@ = (:7:3:);   i.e. x = (.7,6,5,4,3.)
  i: inttuple@ = (.3,6,9.)
ENDDECLARE

lbound@(x)   = 7
rbound@(x)   = 3
isin@(4,x)   = 1   (bool)
arein@(i,x)   = 0   (bool)   (9 is not in range)
position@(6,x) = 2
position@(9,x)   assertion error (9 is not in range)
normalize@(x)   = (:1:5:)   (.1,2,3,4,5.)
ordinal_range@(5) = (:1:5:)   /"

3.7. Array Dimensions

TYPE array_dimension@ BODY
ALL a: tytuple@(range@) WITH size@(a) > 0 ENDALL
                                      "/Array dimensions are lists (tuples) of ranges/"

CARRY equal,notequal,size@,tail@,select@,exchange@,extend@ ENDCARRY

                      "/Is an index within declared bounds ?/"
FUNCTION isin@(z: inttuple@; x: array_dimension@): bool
RETURN IF size@(z) ~ = size@(x) THEN 0
    ELIF size@(z) = 1 THEN range@.isin@(z[.1.],x[.1.])
    ELSE range@.isin@(z[.1.],x[.1.]) & isin@(tail@(z),tail@(x)) ENDIF
ENDisin@

                      "/Return a 1-origin array_dimension/"
FUNCTION normalize@(x: array_dimension@): array_dimension@
RETURN new(fmon@(old(x),range@,range@.normalize@))
ENDnormalize@

FUNCTION size_array@(x: array_dimension@): pint   "/Number of array elements/"
  RETURN IF size@(x) = 1 THEN size@(x[.1.])
        ELSE size@(x[.1.]) * size_array@(tail@(x)) ENDIF
ENDsize_array@

                                             "/Order number of a single array element/"
FUNCTION position@(z: inttuple@; x: array_dimension@): pint
  RETURN IF size@(z) = 1 THEN range@.position@(z[.1.],x[.1.])
     ELSE range@.position@(z[.1.],x[.1.]) +
        (size@(x[.1.]) * (position@(tail@(z),tail@(x))-1)) ENDIF
ENDposition@

                                     "/Make an array_dimension from a pinttuple/"
FUNCTION ordinal_dimension@(z: pinttuple@): array_dimension@
  RETURN new(fmon@(z,range@,ordinal_range@))
ENDordinal_dimension@

FORMAT@
  EXTEND expression_range_list.01 ER = expression_range
  MEANS tuplize@(@1)

  EXTEND expression_range_list.02 ER =
          R expression_range ';' expression_range_list
  MEANS (tuplize@(@1) # @2)

  EXTEND range_list.01 R = '[' expression_range_list ']'
  MEANS new(@1)

  EXTEND unsigned_constant_denotation.07 E = R range_list
ENDFORMAT

ENDarray_dimension@

"/Example:

Assume the following declarations:

DECLARE
 a: array_dimension@ = [1:4;-2:2;4:6;4:1];
 x: inttuple@ = (.1,2,3,4.);
 y: inttuple@ = (.4,-2,5,1.);
 z: inttuple@ = (.2,3,4.)
ENDDECLARE

i.e. a = (.(.1,2,3,4.),(.-2,-1,0,1,2.),(.4,5,6.),(.4,3,2,1.).)

isin@(x,a)	= 0	(3rd element of x not in range)
isin@(y,a)	= 1	
isin@(z,a)	= 0	(z lacks an element)
normalize@(a)	= [1:4;1:5;1:3;1:4]	
size_array@(a)	= 240	(4*5*3*4 = 240)
position@(y,a)	= 204	(4+4*(1+5*(2+3*(4-1)-1)-1) = 204)
ordinal_dimension@(z)	= [1:2;1:3;1:4]	/"

18.8. Indexers

TYPE indexer@ BODY
 ALL a: tytuple@(inttuple@) WITH size@(a) > 0 ENDALL

 CARRY equal,notequal,size@,tail@,select@,exchange@ ENDCARRY

"/Is z in dimension ranges of y ?/"
FUNCTION isin@(z: indexer@; y: array_dimension@): bool
 RETURN IF size@(z) ~ = size@(y) THEN 0
    ELIF size@(z) = 1 THEN range@.arein@(z[.1.],y[.1.])
       ELSE range@.arein@(z[.1.],y[.1.]) & isin@(tail@(z),tail@(y)) ENDIF
ENDisin@

"/A degenerate indexer denotes only one array element/"
FUNCTION degenerate@(z: indexer@): bool
 RETURN IF size@(z) = 1 THEN size@(z[.1.]) = 1
          ELSE size@(z[.1.]) = 1 & degenerate@(tail@(z)) ENDIF
ENDdegenerate@

120

"/Make an element index (inttuple) from a degenerate indexer/"
FUNCTION element_tuple@(z: indexer@): inttuple@
 ASSERT degenerate@(z) ENDASSERT
 RETURN IF size@(z) = 1 THEN z[.1.]
            ELSE z[.1.] # element_tuple@(tail@(z)) ENDIF
ENDelement_tuple@

"/Return number of indices of each dimension/"
FUNCTION size_tuple@(z: indexer@): pinttuple@
 RETURN IF size@(z) = 1 THEN tuplize@(size@(z[.1.]))
       ELSE tuplize@(size@(z[.1.])) # size_tuple@(tail@(z)) ENDIF
ENDsize_tuple@

"/Select one element index of an indexer/"
FUNCTION index_map@(x: pinttuple@; z: indexer@): inttuple@
 ASSERT size@(x) = size@(z), x[.1.] =< size@(z[.1.]) ENDASSERT
 RETURN IF size@(x) = 1 THEN tuplize@(z[.1.][.x[.1.].])
       ELSE tuplize@(z[.1.][.x[.1.].]) # index_map@(tail@(x),tail@(z)) ENDIF
ENDindex_map@

"/Return a 1-origin dimension for a subarray selected by z/"
FUNCTION derived_dimension@(z: indexer@): array_dimension@
 RETURN ordinal_dimension@(size_tuple@(z))
ENDderived_dimension@

FORMAT@
 EXTEND elem_list_expr.01 ER = R expression_1:int

 EXTEND element_list.01 ER = elem_list_expr
 MEANS tuplize@((@1)

 EXTEND element_list.02 ER = elem_list_expr ':' elem_list_expr
 MEANS convert@(THE@ r: range@ WITH lbound@(r) = @1 &
            rbound@(r) = @2 ENDTHE,inttuple@)

 EXTEND element_list.03 ER = elem_list_expr ',' element_list
 MEANS (tuplize@((@1) # @2)

EXTEND element_list.04 R = elem_list_expr ':' elem_list_expr ','
                          element_list
MEANS (convert@(THE@ r: range@ WITH lbound@(r) = @1 &
                rbound@(r) = @2 ENDTHE,inttuple@) # @3)

EXTEND dimension_list.01 ER = element_list
MEANS THE@ y: indexer@ WITH size@(y) = 1 AND y[.1.] = @1 ENDTHE

EXTEND dimension_list.02 ER = R element_list ';' dimension_list
MEANS THE@ y: indexer@ WITH
    size@(y) > 1 AND y[.1.] = @1 AND tail@(y) = @2 ENDTHE

ENDFORMAT
ENDindexer@

SUBTYPE degenerate_indexer@ BODY
 ALL i: indexer@ WITH degenerate@(i) ENDALL
ENDdegenerate_indexer@

SUBTYPE ndegenerate_indexer@ BODY
 ALL i: indexer@ WITH ~degenerate@(i) ENDALL
ENDndegenerate_indexer@

18.9. Arrays

TYPE array@(u: any@) BODY   "/For toolmakers only/"
 ALL y: tuple@ WITH
   size@(y) = 2 AND
   select@(y,1) .< array_dimension@ AND
   select@(y,2) .< tytuple@(u) AND
   size@(convert@(select@(y,2),tytuple@(u)))
       = size_array@(convert@(select@(y,1),array_dimension@))
 ENDALL

FUNCTION dpart@(x: array@(u)): array_dimension@   "/Return dimension part/"
  RETURN convert@(select@(old(x),1),array_dimension@)
ENDdpart@

FUNCTION vpart@(x: array@(u)): tytuple@(u)   "/Return value part/"
  RETURN convert@(select@(old(x),2),tytuple@(u))
ENDvpart@

```
FUNCTION dim_count(x: array@(u)): pint                    "/Number of dimensions/"
  RETURN size@(dpart@(x))
ENDdim_count


FUNCTION lb(x: array@(u); d: pint): int                   "/Left bound of a dimension/"
  ASSERT d =< dim_count(x) ENDASSERT
  RETURN range@.lbound@(dpart@(x)[.d.])
ENDlb

FUNCTION rb(x: array@(u); d: pint): int                   "/Right bound of a dimension/"
  ASSERT d =< dim_count(x) ENDASSERT
  RETURN range@.rbound@(dpart@(x)[.d.])
ENDrb


                                                "/Number of elements in a dimension/"
FUNCTION dim_size(x: array@(u); d: pint): pint
  ASSERT d =< dim_count(x) ENDASSERT
  RETURN size@(dpart@(x)[.d.])
ENDdim_size

FUNCTION vsize@(x: array@(u)): pint                       "/Total number of elements/"
  RETURN size@(vpart@(x))
ENDvsize@


                                   "/Arrays are compatible if they have identical shape/"
FUNCTION compatible(x,y: array@(u)): bool
  RETURN normalize@(dpart@(x)) = normalize@(dpart@(y))
ENDcompatible


                                                      "/Normalize the dimensions/"
FUNCTION normalize(x: array@(u)): array@(u)
  RETURN THE@ a: array@(u) WITH
     vpart@(a) = vpart@(x) & dpart@(a) = normalize@(dpart@(x)) ENDTHE
ENDnormalize


                                  "/Local function used to define select functions/"
PRIVATE FUNCTION extract(x: array@(u); z: inttuple@): u
  ASSERT isin@(z, dpart@(x)) ENDASSERT
  RETURN vpart@(x)[.position@(z,dpart@(x)).]
ENDextract
```

FUNCTION select_element(x: array@(u); z: degenerate_indexer@): u
 ASSERT isin@(z, dpart@(x)) ENDASSERT
 RETURN extract(x, element_tuple@(z))
 FORMAT@
  EXTEND expression_10.11 ER = R expression_10 '[' dimension_list ']'
  MEANS select_element(@1,@2)
 ENDFORMAT
ENDselect_element

PRIVATE FUNCTION reduce_dimension(x: array@(u)): array@(u)
 ASSERT vsize@(x) > 1 ENDASSERT
 BODY
  FUNCTION reduce_array_dimension(y: array_dimension@): array_dimension@
  ASSERT size_array@(y) > 1 ENDASSERT
  RETURN
   IF size@(y) = 1 THEN y
   ELIF size_array@(tail@(y)) = 1
      THEN THE@ z: array_dimension@ WITH
        size@(z) = 1 AND z[.1.] = y[.1.] ENDTHE
   ELIF size@(y[.1.]) = 1 THEN reduce_array_dimension(tail@(y))
   ELSE THE@ z: array_dimension@ WITH
        size@(z) > 1 AND z[.1.] = y[.1.] AND
        tail@(z) = reduce_array_dimension(tail@(y)) ENDTHE
   ENDIF
  ENDreduce_array_dimension
  RETURN THE@ y: array@(u) WITH
        dpart@(y) = reduce_array_dimension(dpart@(x)) &
        vpart@(y) = vpart@(x) ENDTHE
ENDreduce_dimension

```
FUNCTION select_slice(x: array@(u); z: ndegenerate_indexer@): array@(u)
 ASSERT isin@(z, dpart@(x)) ENDASSERT
 BODY
 FUNCTION subscript(y: array@(u); q: ndegenerate_indexer@): array@(u)
  ASSERT isin@(q, dpart@(y)) ENDASSERT
  RETURN THE@ a: array@(u) WITH
      dpart@(a) = derived_dimension@(q) AND
      FORALL@ p: inttuple@ IS
       ~isin@(p,dpart@(a)) OR
       convert@(extract(a,p),univ@) = convert@(extract(y,index_map@(p,q)),univ@) ENDFORALL
     ENDTHE
 ENDsubscript
 RETURN reduce_dimension(subscript(x,z))
 FORMAT@
  EXTEND expression_10.11
  MEANS select_slice(@1,@2)
 ENDFORMAT
ENDselect_slice
```

```
                                                   "/Switch two dimensions/"
FUNCTION transpose(x: array@(u); i,j: pint): array@(u)
 ASSERT i =< dim_count(x) , j =< dim_count(x) ENDASSERT
 RETURN THE@ a: array@(u) WITH
     dpart@(a) = exchange@(dpart@(x),i,j) AND
     FORALL@ p: inttuple@ IS
      ~isin@(p,dpart@(a)) OR
      convert@(extract(a,p),univ@) = convert@(extract(x, exchange@(p,i,j)),univ@) ENDFORALL
    ENDTHE
ENDtranspose
```

```
                          "/Compatible dimension parts and identical value parts/"
FUNCTION equal(x,y: array@(u)): bool
 RETURN  compatible(x,y) & vpart@(x) = vpart@(y)
 FORMAT@
  EXTEND expression_4.02
  MEANS equal(@1,@2)
 ENDFORMAT
ENDequal
```

```
FUNCTION not_equal(x,y: array@(u)): bool
 RETURN ~(x = y)
 FORMAT@
  EXTEND expression_4.03
  MEANS not_equal(@1,@2)
 ENDFORMAT
ENDnot_equal
```

```
                                    "/Generic function -- Binary operations on array elements/"
FUNCTION fbin@(x,y: array@(u); ATT f: FUNCTION (u,u): u): array@(u)
 ASSERT compatible(x,y) ENDASSERT
 RETURN
  THE@ z: array@(u) WITH
  dpart@(z) = normalize@(dpart@(x)) AND
  FORALL@ p: inttuple@ IS
   ~isin@(p,dpart@(z)) OR
   convert@(extract(z,p),univ@)
     = convert@(f(extract(normalize(x),p),extract(normalize(y),p)),univ@) ENDFORALL
  ENDTHE
ENDfbin@
```

```
                                    "/Generic function -- Producing a Boolean Array/"
FUNCTION fbool@(x,y: array@(u); ATT f: FUNCTION(u,u): bool): array@(bool)
 ASSERT compatible(x,y) ENDASSERT
 RETURN
  THE@ z: array@(u) WITH
  dpart@(z) = normalize@(dpart@(x)) AND
  FORALL@ p: inttuple@ IS
   ~isin@(p,dpart@(z)) OR
   convert@(extract(z,p),univ@)
     = convert@(f(extract(normalize(x),p),extract(normalize(y),p)),univ@) ENDFORALL
  ENDTHE
ENDfbool@
```

"/Generic function -- Unary operations on array elements/"
FUNCTION fmon@(x: array@(u); ATT v: any@; ATT f: FUNCTION(u): v): array@(v)
  RETURN THE@ z: array@(v) WITH
      dpart@(z) = normalize@(dpart@(x)) AND
      FORALL@ i: pint IS
        i > vsize@(x) OR
        convert@(vpart@(z)[.i.],univ@) = convert@(f(vpart@(x)[.i.]),univ@)
      ENDFORALL
    ENDTHE
ENDfmon@

"/Generic activity on arrays/"
ACTIVITY abin@(ATT v: any@; W x: array@(u); y: array@(v); ATT g: ACTIVITY(u,v))
  ASSERT compatible(x,y) ENDASSERT
  BODY
  OVER i FROM 1 TO size_array@(dpart@(x))
      REPEAT g(vpart@(x)[.i.], vpart@(y)[.i.]) ENDOVER
ENDabin@

"/Generic activity on an array/"
ACTIVITY amon@(W x: array@(u); ATT g: ACTIVITY(u)) BODY
  OVER i FROM 1 TO size_array@(dpart@(x))
      REPEAT g(vpart@(x)[.i.]) ENDOVER
ENDamon@

FUNCTION cat1(x,y: u): array@(u)
  RETURN THE@ a: array@(u) WITH
      dpart@(a) = [1:2] AND
      convert@(vpart@(a)[.1.],univ@) = convert@(x,univ@) AND
      convert@(vpart@(a)[.2.],univ@) = convert@(y,univ@)
    ENDTHE
  FORMAT@
    EXTEND expression_9.02
    MEANS cat1(@1,@2)
  ENDFORMAT
ENDcat1

```
FUNCTION cat2(x: u; y: array@(u)): array@(u)
 ASSERT dim_count(y) = 1 ENDASSERT
 RETURN THE@ a: array@(u) WITH
      dpart@(a) = ordinal_dimension@(tuplize@(vsize@(y)+1)) AND
      convert@(vpart@(a)[.1.],univ@) = convert@(x,univ@) AND
      tail@(vpart@(a)) = vpart@(y)
    ENDTHE
 FORMAT@
  EXTEND expression_9.02
  MEANS cat2(@1,@2)
 ENDFORMAT
ENDcat2


FUNCTION cat3(x: array@(u); y: u): array@(u)
 ASSERT dim_count(x) = 1 ENDASSERT
 RETURN THE@ a: array@(u) WITH
      dpart@(a) = ordinal_dimension@(tuplize@(vsize@(x)+1)) AND
      vpart@(a) = vpart@(x) # y
    ENDTHE
 FORMAT@
  EXTEND expression_9.02
  MEANS cat3(@1,@2)
 ENDFORMAT
ENDcat3
```

                                              "/Catenation of arrays along one dimension/"
```
FUNCTION catenate(x,y: array@(u); d: pint): array@(u)
 ASSERT dim_count(x) = dim_count(y),
     d =< dim_count(x)+1,
     FORALL@ i: pint IS
      i > dim_count(x) OR i = d OR
      dim_size(x,i) = dim_size(y,i) ENDIF
     ENDFORALL
 ENDASSERT
 BODY
```

                                         "/Add a constant to a position in an element index/"
```
FUNCTION offset(t: inttuple@; p: pint; o: int): inttuple@
 ASSERT p =< size@(t) ENDASSERT
 RETURN IF p = 1 THEN tuplize@(t[.1.]+o) # tail@(t)
          ELSE tuplize@(t[.1.]) # offset(tail@(t),p-1,o) ENDIF
 ENDoffset
```

"/Add a constant to the right boundary of a dimension/"
FUNCTION stretch(t: array_dimension@; p, o: pint): array_dimension@
  RETURN THE@ z: array_dimension@ WITH
      size@(z) = size@(t) AND
      FORALL@ j: pint IS
      j > size@(z) OR
      z[.j.] = IF j ~ = p THEN range@.normalize@(t[.j.])
              ELSE ordinal_range@(size@(t[.j.])+o) ENDIF
      ENDFORALL
      ENDTHE
ENDstretch

RETURN IF d =< dim_count(x) THEN
    THE@ z: array@(u) WITH
    dpart@(z) = stretch(normalize@(dpart@(x)),d,dim_size(y,d)) AND
    FORALL@ p: inttuple@ IS
    ~isin@(p,dpart@(z)) OR
    convert@(extract(z,p),univ@)
    = IF p[.d.] =< dim_size(x,d)
        THEN convert@(extract(normalize(x),p),univ@)
        ELSE convert@(extract(normalize(y), offset(p,d,-dim_size(x,d))),univ@)
                ENDIF
    ENDFORALL
    ENDTHE
    ELSE THE@ z: array@(u) WITH
        dpart@(z) = normalize@(dpart@(x)) # (:1:2:) &
        vpart@(z) = vpart@(x) # vpart@(y)
      ENDTHE
  ENDIF
 FORMAT@
  EXTEND expression_9.02
  MEANS catenate(@1,@2,1)
 ENDFORMAT
ENDcatenate

129

"/Comparison of indexed array elements/"

```
FUNCTION eq(x, y: array@(u)): array@(bool)
  RETURN fbool@(x,y,equal)
  FORMAT@
    EXTEND expression_4.10 = R expression_5 'EQ' expression_5
    MEANS eq(@1,@2)
  ENDFORMAT
ENDeq


FUNCTION neq(x, y: array@(u)): array@(bool)
  RETURN fbool@(x,y,not_equal)
  FORMAT@
    EXTEND expression_4.11 = R expression_5 '~EQ' expression_5
    MEANS neq(@1,@2)
  ENDFORMAT
ENDneq

ENDarray@
```

"/Example:

Assume the following declarations:

```
DECLARE
  a: array@(string)=(. [1:3] , (.'A','B','C'.) .)
  b: array@(string)=(. [-1;1:3] , (.'A','B','C'.) .)
  c: array@(string)=(. [0:1;0:2;0:1] , (.'A','B','C','D','E','F',
                        'G','H','I','J','K','L'.) .)
  d: array@(string)=(. [-1:1], (.'X','Y','C'.) .)
ENDDECLARE
```

```
dpart@(a)        = [1:3]
vpart@(a)        = (.'A','B','C'.)
dim_count(a)     = 1
dim_count(b)     = 2
lb(a,1)        = 1
rb(a,1)        = 3
lb(b,1)        = -1
rb(b,1)        = -1
lb(b,2)        = 1
rb(b,2)        = 3
dim_size(a,1)    = 3
dim_size(b,1)    = 1
dim_size(b,2)    = 3
vsize@(c)        = 12
compatible(a,b)   = 0
compatible(a,d)   = 1
normalize(c)     = (. [1:2;1:3;1:2] , (.'A','B','C','D','E','F',
                         'G','H','I','J','K','L'.) .)

a[1]          = 'A'
b[-1;2]         = 'B'
c[1;0:1;0]      = (. [1:2] , (.'B','D'.) .)
transpose(c,2,3)   = (. [0:1;0:1;0:2] ,(. 'A','B','G','H','C','D',
                         'I','J','E','F','K','L'.) .)
a = b         = 0 (not compatible)
a = d         = 0 (vparts not identical)
a EQ d         = (. [1:3] , (.0,0,1.) .)          /"
```

18.10. Arrays with Fixed Dimensions

SUBTYPE fixed_array@(u: any@; d: array_dimension@) BODY
  ALL x: array@(u) WITH dpart@(x) = d ENDALL
ENDfixed_array@

18.11. Construction of Records

TYPE field_descriptor@ BODY
  ALL x: tuple@ WITH
    size@(x) = 2 AND
    select@(x,1) .< string AND
    designate@(select@(x,2)) .< any@
  ENDALL

"/ A field_descriptor is a 2 element tuple with a field_name as first
and a type identifier as second element/"

CARRY equal,notequal ENDCARRY

FUNCTION name_part@(x: field_descriptor@): string   "/Return field_name/"
  RETURN convert@(select@(old(x),1),string)
ENDname_part@

FUNCTION type_part@(x: field_descriptor@): univ@   "/Return associated type/"
  RETURN select@(old(x),2)
ENDtype_part@

FORMAT@
  EXTEND field_descriptor.01 R = string_denotation ':' type_designator
  MEANS THE@ x: field_descriptor@ WITH
      name_part@(x) = @1 &
      type_part@(x) = @2 ENDTHE
  ENDFORMAT
ENDfield_descriptor@

TYPE field_descriptor_list@ BODY
  ALL x: tytuple@(field_descriptor@) WITH
    FORALL@ i: pint IS
    FORALL@ j: pint IS
    i > size@(x) OR j > size@(x) OR i = j OR
    name_part@(x[.i.]) ~ = name_part@(x[.j.])
    ENDFORALL ENDFORALL
  ENDALL   "/A list of field_descriptors with unique field_names/"

CARRY equal,notequal,select@,size@,tail@ ENDCARRY

                "/Return the position of the field_descriptor with the field_name s/"
FUNCTION field_position@(x: field_descriptor_list@; s: string): pint
  RETURN IF name_part@(x[.1.]) = s THEN 1
      ELSE 1 + field_position@(tail@(x),s) ENDIF
ENDfield_position@

FORMAT@
  EXTEND field_descriptor_list.01 ER = field_descriptor
  MEANS THE@ x: field_descriptor_list@ WITH
      size@(x) = 1 AND x[.1.] = @1 ENDTHE

EXTEND field_descriptor_list.02 R =
      field_descriptor ';' field_descriptor_list
MEANS THE@ x: field_descriptor_list@ WITH
   size@(x) > 1 AND x[.1.] = @1 AND tail@(x) = @2 ENDTHE
ENDFORMAT
ENDfield_descriptor_list@

TYPE record@(u: field_descriptor_list@) BODY
 ALL x: tuple@ WITH
  size@(x) = size@(u) AND
  FORALL@ i: pint IS
  i > size@(x) OR select@(x,i) .< designate@(type_part@(u[.i.]))
  ENDFORALL
 ENDALL

 CARRY equal,notequal ENDCARRY

 FUNCTION record_select(x: record@(u);ATT a: string):
          designate@(type_part@(u[.field_position@(u,a).]))
  RETURN convert@(select@(old(x), field_position@(u,a)),
          designate@(type_part@(u[.field_position@(u,a).])))
  FORMAT@
   EXTEND expression_10.12 ER = R expression_10 '!' string_denotation
   MEANS record_select(@1,@2)
  ENDFORMAT
 ENDrecord_select

 FORMAT@
  EXTEND type_designator.04 E = R 'record' '(' field_descriptor_list ')'
  MEANS (record@(@1))
 ENDFORMAT
ENDrecord

18.12. Computation Step Signals

TYPE cs_signal@(u: any@) BODY
 ALL a: tytuple@(u) WITH size@(a) = 1 | size@(a) = 2 ENDALL

 CARRY equal,notequal,size@ ENDCARRY

```
FUNCTION select_css@(x: cs_signal@(u); s: pint): u
  RETURN old(x)[.s.]
  FORMAT@
    EXTEND expression_10.13 ER = R expression_10 '{' expression_1 '}'
    MEANS select_css@(@1,@2)
  ENDFORMAT
ENDselect_css@
```

"/Extend a computation step signal/"

```
FUNCTION extend_css@(x: cs_signal@(u); v: u): cs_signal@(u)
  RETURN IF size@(x) = 2 THEN new(remove@(old(x),2) # v)
            ELSE new(old(x) # v) ENDIF
ENDextend_css@
```

"/Pack value v to a cs_signal/"

```
FUNCTION pack_css@(v: u): cs_signal@(u)
  RETURN new(tuplize@(v))
ENDpack_css@
```

```
ENDcs_signal@
```

18.13. Real Time Signals

```
EXTERNAL FUNCTION get_t@: int                    "/access function for t@/"
  FORMAT@                                "/Define t@ to invoke get_t@()/"
  EXTEND expression_10.18 ER = R 't@'
  MEANS get_t@()
  ENDFORMAT
ENDget t@
```

```
TYPE signal@(u: any@) BODY
  record('dpart': u; 'spart': tytuple@(cs_signal@(u)))
```

"/no functions carried from record/"

```
FUNCTION equal@(x,y: signal@(u)): bool
  RETURN old(x) = old(y)
ENDequal@
```

```
FUNCTION notequal@(x,y: signal@(u)): bool
 RETURN old(x) ~ = old(y)
ENDnotequal@
```

```
FUNCTION spart@(x: signal@(u)): tytuple@(cs_signal@(u))              "/signal part/"
 RETURN old(x)!'spart'
ENDspart@
```

```
FUNCTION dpart@(x: signal@(u)): u                                   "/default part/"
 RETURN old(x)!'dpart'
ENDdpart@
```

```
FUNCTION slength@(x: signal@(u)): nnint                             "/signal length/"
 RETURN size@(spart@(x))
ENDslength@
```

"/select cs_signal at rt_interval t/"

```
FUNCTION select_rts@(x: signal@(u); t: pint): cs_signal@(u)
 RETURN spart@(x)[.t.]
 FORMAT@                                                            "/write: x{t} to select one cs_signal/"
  EXTEND expression_10.13
  MEANS select_rts@((@1,@2)
 ENDFORMAT
ENDselect_rts@
```

"/Does a value for rt_interval t, step s exist?/"

```
FUNCTION known@(x: signal@(u); t,s: pint): bool
 RETURN slength@(x) >= t & size@(x{t}) >= s
ENDknown@.
```

"/Instantaneous Value/"

```
FUNCTION inst_value@(x: signal@(u); t,s: pint): u
 ASSERT known@(x, t, s) ENDASSERT
 RETURN x{t}{s}
```

```
 FORMAT@
  EXTEND expression_10.14 ER =
       R expression_10 '{' expression_1 ',' expression_1 '}'
  MEANS inst_value@((@1,@2,@3)
```

"/x{t,s} means x{t}{s}/"

EXTEND expression_10.15 ER = R expression_10 '{' expression_10 ',' '}'
MEANS inst_value@(@1,@2,1)

"/x{t,} means first element of cs_signal x{t}/"

EXTEND expression_10.16 ER = R expression_10 '{' '}'
MEANS inst_value@(@1,slength@((@1),1)

"/x{} means first value of present rt_interval/"

ENDFORMAT
ENDinst_value@

"/Return signal x delayed for d rt_intervals/"
FUNCTION delay(x: signal@(u); d: pint): signal@(u)
 RETURN THE@ z: signal@(u) WITH
      convert@(dpart@(z),univ@) = convert@(dpart@(x),univ@) AND
      slength@(z) = slength@(x) AND
      FORALL@ i: pint IS i > slength@(z) OR
       z{i} = IF i > d THEN x{i-d}
              ELSE pack_css@(dpart@(x)) ENDIF
      ENDFORALL ENDTHE
 FORMAT@
  EXTEND expression_7.03 ER = R expression_7 '%' expression_8
  MEANS delay(@1,@2)
 ENDFORMAT
ENDdelay

"/Extend a signal/"
FUNCTION extend_rts@(x: signal@(u); t: pint; v: u): signal@(u)
 ASSERT t = slength@(x) | t = slength@(x)+1 ENDASSERT
 RETURN THE@ z: signal@(u) WITH
      convert@(dpart@(z),univ@) = convert@(dpart@(x),univ@) AND
      slength@(z) = t AND
      FORALL@ i: pint IS i >= t OR z{i} = x{i} ENDFORALL AND
      IF slength@(x) = t THEN z{t} = extend_css@(x{t},v)
              ELSE z{t} = pack_css@(v) ENDIF
    ENDTHE
ENDextend_rts@

```
                                          "/Return a signal where x{} is replaced by c/"
FUNCTION comprint@(x: signal@(u); c: u): signal@(u)
 RETURN THE@ z: signal@(u) WITH
      convert@(dpart@(z),univ@) = convert@(dpart@(x),univ@) AND
      slength@(z) = slength@(x) AND
      FORALL@ i: pint IS
       i >= slength@(z) OR z{i} = x{i} ENDFORALL AND
      z{slength@(z)} = pack_css@(c)
   ENDTHE
ENDcomprint@



                                          "/Generic function: unary operation on signals/"
FUNCTION smon@(x: signal@(u); ATT f: FUNCTION(u): u): signal@(u)
 RETURN THE@ z: signal@(u) WITH
      convert@(dpart@(z),univ@) = convert@(f(dpart@(x)),univ@) AND
      slength@(z) = slength@(x) AND
      FORALL@ i: pint IS
       i > slength@(z) OR z{i} = pack css@(f(x{i,})) ENDFORALL
   ENDTHE
ENDsmon@



                                          "/Generic function: binary operation on signals/"
FUNCTION sbin@(x,y: signal@(u); ATT f: FUNCTION(u,u): u): signal@(u)
 ASSERT slength@(x) = slength@(y) ENDASSERT
 RETURN THE@ z: signal@(u) WITH
      convert@(dpart@(z),univ@) = convert@(f(dpart@(x), dpart@(y)),univ@) AND
      slength@(z) = slength@(x) AND
      FORALL@ i: pint IS
       i > slength@(z) OR z{i} = pack_css@(f(x{i,},y{i,}))
      ENDFORALL
   ENDTHE
ENDsbin@
```

```
                                         "/Generic function: boolean operation on signals/"
FUNCTION sbool@(x,y: signal@(u); ATT f: FUNCTION(u,u): bool): signal@(bool)
  ASSERT slength@(x) = slength@(y) ENDASSERT
  RETURN THE@ z: signal@(u) WITH
       convert@(dpart@(z),univ@) = convert@(f(dpart@(x), dpart@(y)),univ@) AND
       slength@(z) = slength@(x) AND
       FORALL@ i: pint IS
         i > slength@(z) OR z{i} = pack_css@(f(x{i,},y{i,}))
       ENDFORALL
     ENDTHE
ENDsbool@


"/The appearance of a signal s where a value is expected
  invokes interpreter function val(s)/"

INTERPRETER@ FUNCTION val(x: signal@(u)): u
  RETURN x{}
ENDval

"/The appearance of a value v where a signal is expected
  invokes interpreter function pack(v)/"

INTERPRETER@ FUNCTION pack(v: u): signal@(u)
  RETURN THE@ z: signal@(u) WITH
       convert@(dpart@(z),univ@) = convert@(v,univ@)  AND
       slength@(z) = t@ AND
       FORALL@ i: pint IS
         i > t@ OR z{i} = pack_css@(v) ENDFORALL
     ENDTHE
  ENDpack

ENDsignal@

TYPE signal(u: val_type) BODY
  signal@(u)
  CARRYALL
ENDsignal
```

18.14. Class of Signal Types

CLASS sig_type BODY
  ALL x: any@ WITH x <| class_signal ENDALL
ENDsig_type

18.15. Carriers

TYPE terminal@(u: any@; def: u; cd: bool) BODY
  cell@(signal@(u))

  PRIVATE FUNCTION get@(x: terminal@(u,df,cd)): signal@(u)
    RETURN IF empty@(old(x)) THEN pack(def)   "/Initialization/"
            ELSE get@(old(x)) ENDIF
  ENDget@

  INTERPRETER@ FUNCTION val(x: terminal@(u,def,cd)): u
    RETURN get@(x){}
  ENDval

  INTERPRETER@ FUNCTION sig(x: terminal@(u,def,cd)): signal@(u)
      RETURN comprint@(get@(x),val(x))
  ENDsig

  ACTIVITY connect(W x: terminal@(u,def,cd); a: u)
    ASSERT ~cd OR ~known@(get@(x),t@,2) OR get@(x){t@,2} = a ENDASSERT
    BODY put@(old(x), extend_rts@(get@(x),t@,a))

    FORMAT@
      EXTEND simple_activity_invocation.02 E
                  = R expression_1 '.=' expression_1
      MEANS connect(@1,@2)
    ENDFORMAT
  ENDconnect

  INTERPRETER@ ACTIVITY finstep(W x: terminal@(u,def,cd)) BODY
    IF ~known@(get@(x),t@,2) THEN connect(x,def) ENDIF
  ENDfinstep

  INTERPRETER@ ACTIVITY finint(W x: terminal@(u,def,cd)) BODY
    put@(old(x), extend_rts@(get@(x),t@+1,get@(x){}))
  ENDfinint

```
INTERPRETER@ ACTIVITY shrink(W x: terminal@(u,def,cd)) BODY
 put@(old(x), comprint@(get@(x),get@(x){t@,2})
ENDshrink


INTERPRETER@ ACTIVITY setlength(W x: terminal@(u,def,cd))
 ASSERT slength@(get@(x)) =< t@ ENDASSERT
 BODY  put@(old(x), THE@ z: signal@(u) WITH
            convert@(dpart@(z),univ@) = convert@(def,univ@) AND
            slength@(z) = t@ AND
            FORALL@ i: pint IS
             IF i =< slength@(get@(x))
               THEN z{i} = get@(x){i}
             ELIF i =< t@ THEN z{i} = pack_css@(def)
             ELSE 1 ENDIF
            ENDFORALL ENDTHE)
  ENDsetlength
ENDterminal@

TYPE terminal(u: val_type; def: u) BODY
 terminal@(u,def,1)
 CARRYALL
ENDterminal

SUBTYPE btml(default: bool) BODY terminal(bool, default) ENDbtml
SUBTYPE btm0 BODY btml(0) ENDbtm0
SUBTYPE btm1 BODY btml(1) ENDbtm1

SUBTYPE itml(default: int) BODY terminal(int,default) ENDitml

TYPE variable@(u: any@; def: u; cd: bool) BODY
 cell@(signal@(u))

PRIVATE FUNCTION get@(x: variable@(u,df,cd)): signal@(u)
 RETURN IF empty@(old(x)) THEN pack(def)
            ELSE get@(old(x)) ENDIF
ENDget@

INTERPRETER@ FUNCTION val(x: variable@(u,def,cd)): u
 RETURN get@(x){}
ENDval
```

"/Initialization/"

```
INTERPRETER@ FUNCTION sig(x: variable@(u,def,cd)): signal@(u)
    RETURN comprint@(get@(x),val(x))
ENDsig


ACTIVITY assign(W x: variable@(u,def,cd); a: u)
  ASSERT ~cd OR ~known@(get@(x),t@,2) OR get@(x){t@,2} = a ENDASSERT
  BODY  put@(old(x), extend_rts@(get@(x),t@,a))

 FORMAT@
  EXTEND simple_activity_invocation.03 E
                   = R expression_1 ':=' expression_1
  MEANS assign(@1,@2)
 ENDFORMAT
ENDassign

INTERPRETER@ ACTIVITY finstep(W x: variable@(u,def,cd)) BODY
 IF ~known@(get@(x),t@,2) THEN assign(x,val(x)) ENDIF
ENDfinstep

INTERPRETER@ ACTIVITY finint(W x: variable@(u,def,cd)) BODY
 put@(old(x), extend_rts@(get@(x),t@+1,get@(x){}))
ENDfinint

INTERPRETER@ ACTIVITY shrink(W x: variable@(u,def,cd)) BODY
 put@(old(x), comprint@(get@(x),get@(x){t@,2})
ENDshrink

INTERPRETER@ ACTIVITY setlength(W x: variable@(u,def,cd))
 ASSERT slength@(get@(x)) =< t@ ENDASSERT
 BODY  put@(old(x), THE@ z: signal@(u) WITH
               convert@(dpart@(z),univ@) = convert@(def,univ@) AND
               slength@(z) = t@ AND
               FORALL@ i: pint IS
                 IF i =< slength@(get@(x))
                   THEN z{i} = get@(x){i}
                   ELIF i =< t@ THEN z{i} = pack_css@(val(x))
                   ELSE 1 ENDIF
                 ENDFORALL ENDTHE)
ENDsetlength


ENDvariable@
```

TYPE variable(u: val_type; def: u) BODY
 variable@(u,def,1)
 CARRYALL
ENDvariable

SUBTYPE bvar(init: bool) BODY variable(bool,init) ENDbvar

SUBTYPE ivar(init: int) BODY variable(int,init) ENDivar

TYPE rtvariable@(u: any@; def: u; cd: bool) BODY
 cell@(signal@(u))

 PRIVATE FUNCTION get@(x: rtvariable@(u,df,cd)): signal@(u)
  RETURN IF empty@(old(x)) THEN pack(def)   "/Initialization/"
            ELSE get@(old(x)) ENDIF
 ENDget@

 INTERPRETER@ FUNCTION val(x: rtvariable@(u,def,cd)): u
  RETURN IF slength@(get@(x)) = 1 THEN def
       ELSE get@(x){slength@(get@(x))-1,} ENDIF
 ENDval

 INTERPRETER@ FUNCTION sig(x: rtvariable@(u,def,cd)): signal@(u)
    RETURN comprint@(get@(x),val(x))
 ENDsig

 ACTIVITY transfer(W x: rtvariable@(u,def,cd); a: u)
  ASSERT ~cd OR ~known@(get@(x),t@,2) OR get@(x){t@,2} = a ENDASSERT
  BODY put@(old(x), extend_rts@(get@(x),t@,a))

 FORMAT@
   EXTEND simple_activity_invocation.04 E
                = R expression_1 '<-' expression_1
   MEANS transfer(@1,@2)
  ENDFORMAT
 ENDtransfer

 INTERPRETER@ ACTIVITY finstep(W x: rtvariable@(u,def,cd)) BODY
  IF ~known@(get@(x),t@,2) THEN transfer(x,val(x)) ENDIF
 ENDfinstep

INTERPRETER@ ACTIVITY finint(W x: rtvariable@(u,def,cd)) BODY
  put@(old(x), extend_rts@(get@(x),t@+1,get@(x){}))
ENDfinint

INTERPRETER@ ACTIVITY shrink(W x: rtvariable@(u,def,cd)) BODY
  put@(old(x), comprint@(get@(x),get@(x){t@,2}))
ENDshrink

INTERPRETER@ ACTIVITY setlength(W x: rtvariable@(u,def,cd))
  ASSERT slength@(get@(x)) =< t@ ENDASSERT
  BODY put@(old(x), THE@ z: signal@(u) WITH
          convert@(dpart@(z),univ@) = convert@(def,univ@) AND
          slength@(z) = t@ AND
          FORALL@ i: pint IS
           IF i =< slength@(get@(x))
             THEN z{i} = get@(x){i}
           ELIF i =< t@ THEN z{i} = pack_css@(val(x))
           ELSE 1 ENDIF
          ENDFORALL ENDTHE)
  ENDsetlength

ENDrtvariable@

TYPE rtvariable(u: val_type; def: u) BODY
  rtvariable@(u,def,1)
  CARRYALL
ENDrtvariable

SUBTYPE brtv(init: bool) BODY rtvariable(bool,init) ENDbrtv

18.16. Class of Carrier Types

CLASS carr_type BODY
  ALL x: any@ WITH
    x <| class_terminal |
    x <| class_variable |
    x <| class_rtvariable
  ENDALL
ENDcarr_type

ENDbcl

19. Bcl Model of Computation

19.1. Modelling the time behavior of a description written in CONLAN

19.1.1. Stabilization of a Description

Chapter 15 describing the semantics of pscl in terms of the Worker Model provides the basic mechanisms by which a text written in Primitive Set CONLAN can be interpreted. These mechanisms ensure that all activity invocation statements are evaluated concurrently, so that the order in which they have been written has no impact on the result. The bcl model of time has not yet been introduced and single values are stored into the cells.

The notion of history of values comes with the definition of computation_step_signals (type cs_signal@) and time_signals (type signal@) in Base CONLAN. When modelling digital hardware, computation_step_signals correspond to transient values, due to the propagation of a state change in the system; this propagation is supposed to take a physical time so small with respect to the chosen unit of time that its duration is neglected, and possible intermediate values in the carriers are invisible to the hardware designer: only final values have significance. Successive observable values in the carriers are therefore final values of successive cs_signals. In CONLAN, time_signals are those sequences of cs_signals along time. Time_signals can only be inspected by the user for their past and present final values; however, in order to support the test for stability, also the previous step value is supposed to be retained in the carriers, during present time evaluation.

In the following it will be assumed that all carriers declared in a DESCRIPTION segment to be interpreted at the Base CONLAN level, or written in any CONLAN language defined after Base CONLAN, contain time-signals. Such carriers are members of class carr_type.

Stabilization of a segment in bcl is the mechanism by which final values at a given time are obtained for all the carriers of that segment (unless that segment oscillates). One or more evaluation steps are performed on that segment. At each step, the current cs_signal of each carrier is updated with one value. A carrier is locally stable when the value added to its cs_signal is equal to the previous one. Segment stability is attained when all carriers are stable simultaneously.

19.1.2. The bcl Step

One step of evaluation of a description is defined to consist of calculating concurrently all activities invoked in the body of the description exactly once. At the pscl level (REFLAN pscl), "calculation" means one evaluation of each activity invocation. At the bcl level (REFLAN bcl), "calculation" means stabilization of all nonprimitive activities. Primitive bcl activities .=, := and <- stabilize immediately due to the fact that they are defined in pscl. Consider an non-primitive operation counting the "ones" in a Boolean vector written as a FUNCTION and as an ACTIVITY segment with REFLAN bcl:

```
FUNCTION count_ones(x: array@(bvar(0))): pint
 ASSERT dim_count(x) = 1 & lb(x,1) < rb(x,1) ENDASSERT
 BODY DECLARE i,r: ivar(0) ENDDECLARE
  IF i < dim_size(x,1) THEN i: = i + 1 ENDIF;
  IF i < dim_size(x,1) AND x[lb(x,1)+i] THEN r: = r + 1 ENDIF;
 RETURN r
ENDcount_ones
```

```
ACTIVITY counting_ones(W r: ivar(0); x: array@(bvar(0)))
 ASSERT dim_count(x) = 1 & lb(x,1) < rb(x,1) ENDASSERT
 BODY DECLARE i: ivar(0) ENDDECLARE
 IF i < dim_size(x,1) THEN i: = i + 1 ENDIF;
 IF i < dim_size(x,1) AND x[lb(x,1)+i] THEN r: = r + 1 ENDIF
ENDcounting_ones
```

Suppose these segments are invoked inside appropriate description segments.

```
DESCRIPTION d1(IN b: fixed_array@(bvar(0),[1:8]); .... )
.....
DECLARE a: itml(0) ENDDECLARE
.....
a. = count_ones(b);
.....
ENDd1
```

```
DESCRIPTION d2(IN b: fixed_array@(bvar(0),[1:8]); .... )
.....
DECLARE a: ivar(0) ENDDECLARE
.....
counting_ones(a,b);
.....
ENDd2
```

Then, at every calculation step for the evaluation of description d1, the primitive connect activity to terminal "a" and, in conjunction with it, the evaluation of the function "count_ones" is invoked exactly once. The evaluation of this function for the specified 8 bit vector "b" takes 9 local calculation steps until it stabilizes and is ready to return its result to the connect activity for one step of evaluation at the description level.

Similary, at every calculation step for description d2, the activity "counting_ones" is invoked exactly only once. For each such invocation 9 local calculation steps must be executed to obtain stabilization in output variable "a" as a prerequisite for the execution of the next calculation step at the description level. Therefore, stabilization of a whole DESCRIPTION segment is obtained by local stabilization, at each step, of all FUNCTION and ACTIVITY segments invoked in the description. Invoked operations require local step counters to achieve this effect. When the whole description has been stabilized at a given time, all intermediate step values are suppressed: only the final observable value for that time is kept in each carrier of the description.

19.2. Additional Mechanisms at the Base CONLAN Level

19.2.1. Global Time and Step Counters
Two objects, 't@' and 's@', of type cell@(int) are created at compile time, together with all the permanent workers. These cells may be written by the environment only; their capability contains a single element, the environment. All instances of description workers have read access to t@ through the access function "get_t@".

19.2.2. Local Step Counters
Each user defined FUNCTION or ACTIVITY segment receives from the compiler, in addition to all parameter and locally declared carriers, a local step counter of type cell@(int), which will be denoted 'ls@'. This local step counter is hired by each worker associated with an operation segment during his initialization stage. 'ls@' is used to count the number of evaluation steps necessary to stabilize the operation segment, for one invocation. 'ls@' is initialized with the value "1" when the corresponding operation worker receives an EVAL or COMPUTE message.

19.2.3. Additions to an Operation Task
For any operation definition segment, a task of evaluation is elaborated by the compiler. This task includes, at the pscl level, hiring of all local carrier and operation workers, the parameter matching actions, and knowledge of the sequence of message exchanges to be performed during the dynamic evaluation stages.

In addition to this list the task of evaluation at the bcl level includes hiring of the local step counter, hiring of operation workers not explicitly invoked in the operation segment (finstep, shrink and setlength), and a number of tests and termination actions. In particular, the compiler assigns to the operation evaluation task a limit on the number of calculation steps.

In the following, the principles of a pscl operation evaluation are assumed, and only the differences between bcl and pscl evaluations are elaborated. In particular, processing ATT parameters and imported objects is done identically, and will not be repeated here.

19.3. Evaluation of Operations at the bcl Level

19.3.1. Functions
Let 'f' be a user defined function. Evaluation of f is initiated when the worker attached to f receives the message:

$$w: COMPUTE(p1,p2,....,pn) \rightarrow f$$

Parameter Evaluation

All parameters are evaluated as specified in pscl (Section 15.2.3.3). This includes at the bcl level also the evaluation of the parameter matching functions, which have been automatically inserted at compile time (Section 17.3.3). If an error condition exists, an ERROR message is issued.

If assertions are written about the parameters in the operation definition, hire for each asserted boolean expression a worker capable of evaluating it, and send concurrently to all these workers a COMPUTE message. If at least one RESULT message contains <u>false</u>, an ERROR message is issued.

Otherwise, replace in the BODY (if there is one) and the RETURN expression all the occurences of the non-carrier formal parameters with the result of the evaluation of their corresponding actual parameter. Proceed to BODY Evaluation.

BODY Evaluation

If the function segment has no BODY part, proceed to RETURN Expression Evaluation. If no internal carrier is declared, proceed to phase 2.

Phase 1
Obtain a fresh cell@(int) which will be the local step counter and initialize it with 1. If the function is dynamic, and if internal carriers are declared, obtain fresh, empty carriers of the specified type, and attached workers, by issuing for each a SEND message to the recruiter. If the function is static, all local carriers are already there. However, through the combined effects of nested and conditional invocations, the length of the signal held in local carriers might be different to t@. Initialize each local carrier to the proper signal, by invoking activity setlength on each one. For one carrier, the sequence of messages is the following:

f: SEND(setlength) -> recruiter

+

f <- recruiter: RECEIVE(wsetlength)

+

f: id, EVAL(carrier_name) -> wsetlength

+

f <- wsetlength: EVALUATED

+

f: START -> wsetlength

+

f <- wsetlength: DONE

Then proceed to phase 2.

Phase 2
If the BODY has no operation invocation, proceed to RETURN Expression Evaluation. If the BODY has an operation invocation part, then it amounts to a list of conditional or unconditional activity invocations. For each dynamic invocation, hire a worker capable of executing it. Send an EVAL message to each worker, with its actual parameters.

If at least one ERROR message is returned, issue an ERROR message to the caller, with all explanations. Fire all workers hired for this evaluation and stop. If all workers have transmitted an EVALUATED message, send to all of them a START message.

If at least one ERROR message is returned, issue an ERROR message to the caller; fire all workers hired for this evaluation and stop. Otherwise, when all DONE messages have been received, one step of evaluation of the function body has been completed. Fire all activity workers hired during this phase. Then, for each (W parameter or locally declared) carrier, hire a worker capable of interpreting activity finstep. Send concurrently EVAL messages with the associated carrier name to all the finstep, and after receiving all EVALUATED answers send them START messages. When all DONE messages have been received, fire all the finstep workers.

Add 1 into ls@, and test all carriers for stability, which for a given carrier 'ca' consists of evaluating the expression:

$$get@(ca)\{t@, 1\} = get@(ca)\{t@, 2\}$$

If all carriers have stabilized, proceed to phase 3. Otherwise, if the number of evaluation steps performed for the function has reached the limit fixed by the compiler, issue an ERROR message, fire all workers hired for this evaluation, and stop.

If the function has not attained stability, but evaluation cycles are still permitted, hire for each W parameter or locally declared carrier a worker capable of interpreting activity "shrink" and perform the same procedure as with "finstep". After this repeat this phase.

Phase 3   Hire for each W parameter or locally declared carrier a worker capable of interpreting activity "shrink" and perform the same procedure as with "finstep". If assertions are written about local carriers in the BODY of the function segment, hire for each asserted boolean expression a worker to evaluate it; COMPUTE messages are sent concurrently to all these workers. If at least one RESULT message contains false, return an ERROR message to the caller; fire all workers hired for this evaluation and stop.

If no assertion was written, or if all assertions have returned true, proceed to RETURN Expression Evaluation.

RETURN Expression Evaluation

Evaluate the RETURN expression, by hiring a worker w capable of computing the outer function of this expression put in prefix notation, and sending him the message

$$f: COMPUTE(a1, a2, ...am) \rightarrow w$$

The obtained answer, whether it is an ERROR or a RESULT message, is transmitted by the function to his caller. Fire all workers hired for this evaluation and stop.

19.3.2. Activities

Let 'act' be a user defined activity. Evaluation of act is divided in two main stages, corresponding to the EVAL - EVALUATED and the START - DONE pairs of messages.

Parameter Evaluation

Upon receipt of the message

$$w:\ id,\ EVAL(p1,\ p2,\ ...\ pn)\ \text{->}\ act$$

act evaluates concurrently all the parameters as specified in pscl (Section 15.2.3.3). If an error condition exists, an ERROR message is issued. If assertions are written about the parameters in the operation definition, act hires for each asserted boolean expression a worker capable of evaluating it, and sends concurrently to all these workers a COMPUTE message. If at least one RESULT message contains _false_, an ERROR message is issued. For each formal carrier parameter and each imported carrier with W access right hire a carrier of the specified type and copy the signal held by the actual carrier into this carrier. If no error condition exists, act replaces in its BODY all occurrences of the non-carrier formal parameters with the result of the evaluation of their corresponding actual parameters, and sends back an EVALUATED message.

Activity Execution

Upon receipt of the message

$$w:\ START\ \text{->}\ act$$

if the BODY has no operation invocation part, act returns a DONE message to its caller. Otherwise, the processes of hiring and initializing local carriers, invoking internal operations and stabilizing all carriers, and verifying assertions on local and parameter carriers are respectively identical to phases 1, 2 and 3 of function BODY evaluation.

If no ERROR message is issued during these phases,stable values are obtained in all carriers known by act. However, the number of steps taken by act to stabilize should have no influence on his caller. This statement implies that the signal held by W carrier parameters and W imported carriers should not have grown by more than one element. This effect is obtained by passing back to the actual parameter just the last value of the current cs signal held by the formal. Finally act issues a DONE message to his caller, fires all workers hired for this evaluation and stops.

19.4. Evaluation of Instances of DESCRIPTION in bcl

Instances of DESCRIPTION have the same behavior at the Base CONLAN level as the one described at the pscl level. Their effect is to transmit messages and to modify the context attached to the messages. A whole description is therefore stabilized globally, under the control of the environment. Together with it, the compiler has fixed a limit on the number of evaluation steps permitted at any time: if the carriers do not stabilize within this limit, the description is unstable. This limit is communicated to the environment.

All other compile time actions have been already explained at length, and take place before dynamic evaluation is started. The dynamic evaluation of a description starts at $t@=1$ and $s@=1$. It consists of the following stages:

Stage 1

The environment sends an EVAL message to the outer instance of DESCRIPTION worker. Let's assume its name is 'descr'; descr in turn sends EVAL messages to all its local ACTIVITY and instances of DESCRIPTION workers, and the process is repeated down the tree of nested instances.

When the environment receives from descr the EVALUATED message, It sends a START message to descr. This message is also forwarded down the tree of nested instances. When all DONE message have climbed up the tree again, and the environment receives a DONE message from descr, advance to stage 2. If instead of the EVALUATED or the DONE message, the environment receives an ERROR message, the environment may decide to stop the evaluation, or to modify the value of one or more carriers of the description, and resume at the beginning of stage 1.

Stage 2

The environment invokes finstep on all the carriers of the description and of all nested instances, all the carriers which it knows and on which it has a write access.

The environment increases by 1 the step counter $s@$. Then all known carriers are checked for stability. If one or more carriers have differing last values in their current cs_signals and $s@$ is less than the predetermined limit, invoke shrink on all carriers and return to stage 1. If $s@$ equals the predetermined limit, publish an "oscillation" error, and either continue with stage 3 or stop. If all carriers are stable, proceed to stage 3.

Stage 3

The environment invokes shrink and finint on all the carriers of the description which it knows. Then, depending upon the value of $t@$, and the number of simulation time intervals that the user requested, the environment may decide to stop, or to continue evaluation. If continuation is elected, the environment increases the value of $t@$ by 1, sets $s@$ to 1 and returns to stage 1.

V Pscl and Bcl Syntax

In this part of the report we present the combined syntax of pscl and bcl. Those constructs provided by bcl are clearly identified. They were introduced via syntax modification statements during the development of bcl.

As is customary in the presentation of programming language syntax we use an extension of the Backus-Naur-Form (BNF). We depart from the norm however in that we do not tend to reduce the size of the grammar by introducing auxiliary productions for commonly used parts of rules. Thus, the reader will notice that syntactically identical rules may appear several times under different names. The motivation is to keep bcl (and pscl) constructs as self contained as possible. This makes it easier to modify the syntax when deriving new languages since the toolmakers will then not have to be concerned with unintended side-effects which might ensue from the elimination of a rule being used in several places.

20. Meta Notation

Productions have the following form:

> restrictions production_name
> = alternative_list .

Nonterminal symbols are written as simple identifiers. Terminal symbols are strings of characters bound by apostrophes. If an apostrophe appears within a terminal, it is written doubled.

An alternative_list consists of one or more alternatives, which are separated by '|', and an instance of an alternative_list selects exactly one of the list's alternatives.

An alternative consists of terminals, nonterminals and nested alternative_lists, using three kinds of structuring:

1. Syntactic repetition means zero or more instances of the enclosed alternative_list and is denoted by '{' and '}' .

2. Syntactic option means zero or one instance and is denoted by '[' and ']'.

3. Syntactic grouping means exactly one instance and is denoted by '(' and ')'.

The main alternatives of a production are numbered with unique integers, thus providing the addressing mechanism used in FORMAT@ statements.

The application of FORMAT@ statements is limited by restrictions ('E' and 'R') which are attached to production_names and main alternatives. Their semantic is explained together with the FORMAT@ statement.

Some additional information,which cannot be expressed syntactically, is provided via "attribute_tags" appended to nonterminals. An attribute_tag is an identifier prefixed with ':' . For example, expression : int_constant

indicates that only a constant (=compile time) expression of type int can appear in this context.

To enhance readability and support implementation there are several kinds of identifiers in the syntax (e.g. constant_identifier, function_identifier, description_identifier, etc.), which are syntactically identical. Their distinction must be accomplished by symboltable management. Where a new identifier is introduced (nonterminal "identifier" in the syntax), an attribute_tag is given which shows, how this identifier will be handled furtheron. For example,

identifier : def_function

means that this identifier will be recognized further on as a function_identifier.

General commentary information is enclosed in '"/' and '/"' .

21. Syntax

21.1. Language Root

E bcl
    = R 01 reflan_prefix conlan_segment
    | 02 reflan_prefix description_segment
    | R 03 reflan_prefix function_segment
    | R 04 reflan_prefix activity_segment
    | R 05 reflan_prefix interpreter_or_static function_segment
    | R 06 reflan_prefix interpreter_or_static activity_segment .

  reflan_prefix
    = 01 'REFLAN' language_identifier .

21.2. Basic Symbols

  character
    = 01 any .   "/ any ISO 646-IRV character /"

  digit
    = '0' | '1' | '2' | '3' | '4' | '5' | '6' | '7' | '8' | '9' .

  letter
    = 'a' | 'b' | 'c' | 'd' | 'e' | 'f' | 'g' | 'h' | 'i' | 'j' |
     'k' | 'l' | 'm' | 'n' | 'o' | 'p' | 'q' | 'r' | 's' | 't' |
     'u' | 'v' | 'w' | 'x' | 'y' | 'z' .

identifier
  = 01 letter { ['_'] (letter | digit) }
  | R 02 letter { ['_'] (letter | digit) } '@' .

object_identifier
  = 01 identifier
  | R 02 identifier '.' object_identifier .

type_identifier
  = 01 object_identifier:type .

R class_identifier
  = 01 object_identifier:class .

R function_identifier
  = 01 object_identifier:function .

R activity_identifier
  = 01 object_identifier:activity .

R description_identifier
  = 01 object_identifier:description .

R language_identifier
  = 01 object_identifier:language .

R instance_identifier
  = 01 object_identifier:instance .

end_identifier
  = 01 'END' identifier .

comment
  = 01 '"/' { character } '/"' .

R declared_identifier
  = 01 object_identifier
  | R 02 instance_identifier
      '[' use_expr { ',' use_expr } ']' '.' object_identifier
  | R 03 instance_identifier '.' object_identifier .

identifier_list
  = 01 identifier
  | 02 identifier ',' identifier_list .

21.3. Constant Denotation

ER constant_denotation
  = 01 unsigned_constant_denotation
  | R 02 '+' integer_denotation
  | R 03 '-' integer_denotation .

E unsigned_constant_denotation
  = R 01 integer_denotation
  | R 02 boolean_denotation
  | R 03 string_denotation
  | R 04 tuple_denotation
  | R 05 object_identifier:constant
  | R 06 range_denotation   "/ bcl /"
  | R 07 range_list .   "/ bcl /"

R constant_denotation_list
  = 01 constant_denotation
  | 02 constant_denotation ',' constant_denotation_list .

ER integer_denotation
  = R 01 decimal_denotation
  | R 02 binary_denotation
  | R 03 octal_denotation
  | R 04 hexadecimal_denotation .

ER decimal_denotation
  = R 01 digit { digit } .

ER binary_denotation
  = R 01 ('0' | '1') { '0' | '1' } 'B' .

ER octal_denotation
  = R 01 ('0' | '1' | '2' | '3' | '4' | '5' | '6' | '7')
        { '0' | '1' | '2' | '3' | '4' | '5' | '6' | '7' } 'O' .

ER hexadecimal_denotation
   = R 01 (digit | 'A' | 'B' | 'C' | 'D' | 'E' | 'F')
      { digit | 'A' | 'B' | 'C' | 'D' | 'E' | 'F' } 'H' .

ER boolean_denotation
   = R 01 '0'
   | R 02 '1' .

R string_denotation
   = 01 '"' { character | '""' } '"' .

R tuple_denotation
   = 01 '(.' constant_denotation_list '.)' .

R range_denotation
   = 01 '(:' expression_range ':)' .   "/ bcl /"

R range_list
   = 01 '[' expression_range_list ']' .   "/ bcl /"

ER expression_range_list
   = 01 expression_range   "/ bcl /"
   | R 02 expression_range ';' expression_range_list . "/ bcl /"

R expression_range
   = 01 range_expr ':' range_expr .   "/ bcl /"

ER range_expr
   = R 01 expression_1:int_constant .   "/ bcl /"

ER dimension_list
   = 01 element_list   "/ bcl /"
   | R 02 element_list ';' dimension_list .   "/ bcl /"

R element_list
   = 01 elem_list_expr   "/ bcl /"
   | 02 elem_list_expr ':' elem_list_expr   "/ bcl /"
   | 03 elem_list_expr ',' element_list   "/ bcl /"
   | 04 elem_list_expr ':' elem_list_expr ','
      element_list .   "/ bcl /"

ER elem_list_expr
   = R 01 expression_1:int .   "/ bcl /"

R field_descriptor
   = 01 string_denotation ':' type_designator .   "/ bcl /"

R field_descriptor_list
   = 01 field_descriptor   "/ bcl /"
   | 02 field_descriptor ';' field_descriptor_list .   "/ bcl /"

E type_designator
   = 01 type_identifier
   | R 02 type_identifier '(' type_actual_attribute_list ')'
   | R 03 'record' '(' field_descriptor_list ')' .   "/ bcl /"

R type_actual_attribute_list
   = 01 type_act_att_expr
   | 02 type_act_att_expr ',' type_actual_attribute_list .

ER type_act_att_expr
   = R 01 expression_1:constant_or_type .

R class_designator
   = 01 class_identifier
   | R 02 class_identifier '(' class_actual_attribute_list ')' .

R generic_designator
   = R 01 class_designator
   | R 02 'ACTIVITY' ['(' access_right_and_type_desig_list ')']
   | R 03 'FUNCTION' ['(' type_designator_list ')'] ':'
      type_designator .

R type_designator_list
   = 01 type_designator
   | 02 type_designator ',' type_designator_list .

R access_right_and_type_desig_list
   = 01 ['W'] type_designator
   | 02 ['W'] type_designator ',' access_right_and_type_desig_list .

R class_actual_attribute_list
 = 01 class_act_att_expr
 | 02 class_act_att_expr ',' class_actual_attribute_list .

ER class_act_att_expr
 = R 01 expression_1:constant_or_type .

21.4. Segments

R external_segment_f_a
 = R 01 'EXTERNAL' 'FUNCTION' identifier_list:def_function
  ('ENDEXTERNAL' | 'END')
 | R 02 'EXTERNAL' 'ACTIVITY' identifier_list:def_activity
  ('ENDEXTERNAL' | 'END') .

R external_segment_f_a_d
 = R 01 'EXTERNAL' 'FUNCTION' identifier_list:def_function
  ('ENDEXTERNAL' | 'END')
 | R 02 'EXTERNAL' 'ACTIVITY' identifier_list:def_activity
  ('ENDEXTERNAL' | 'END')
 | R 03 'EXTERNAL' 'DESCRIPTION' identifier_list:def_description
  ('ENDEXTERNAL' | 'END') .

R interpreter_or_static
 = R 01 'INTERPRETER@'
 | R 02 'STATIC'
 | R 03 'INTERPRETER@' 'STATIC' .

21.4.1. Function

R function_segment
 = 01 'FUNCTION' function_header 'RETURN' function_return_part
  ('END' | end_identifier)
 | R 02 'FUNCTION' function_header function_body 'RETURN'
  function_return_part ('END' | end_identifier) .

R function_header
 = 01 identifier:def_function ['(' function_formal_list ')']
  ':' type_or_class_designator_expr
 | R 02 identifier:def_function ['(' function_formal_list ')']
  ':' type_or_class_designator_expr assertions .

R function_body
= 01 'BODY' { function_locals }
| R 02 'BODY' { function_locals } activity_invocation_list
| R 03 'BODY' { function_locals } activity_invocation_list
    assertions .

R function_locals
= R 01 assertions
| R 02 type_segment
| R 03 subtype_segment
| R 04 class_segment
| R 05 external_segment_f_a
| R 06 function_segment
| R 07 activity_segment
| R 08 interpreter_or_static function_segment
| R 09 interpreter_or_static activity_segment
| R 10 declare_statement
| R 11 function_import_statement .

R function_return_part
= 01 return_expr
| R 02 return_expr format_statement_list .

ER return_expr
= R 01 expression_1 .

ER type_or_class_designator_expr
= R 01 expression_1:type_or_class_designator .

R function_formal_list
= 01 function_formal_sublist
| 02 function_formal_sublist ';' function_formal_list .

R function_formal_sublist
= 01 function_formal_input_sublist
| R 02 'ATT' function_formal_attribute_sublist .

R function_formal_input_sublist
= 01 identifier_list:def_object ':' type_designator .

R function_formal_attribute_sublist
    = 01 identifier_list:def_object ':' type_designator
    | R 02 identifier_list:def_type_or_function_or_activity
       ':' generic_designator .

R function_import_statement
    = 01 'IMPORT' import_identifier_list ('ENDIMPORT' | 'END') .

R import_identifier_list
    = 01 declared_identifier [',' import_identifier_list] .

21.4.2. Activity

R activity_segment
    = 01 'ACTIVITY' activity_header 'BODY' { activity_locals }
      activity_invocations_part ('END' | end_identifier) .

R activity_header
    = 01 identifier:def_activity ['(' activity_formal_list ')']
    | R 02 identifier:def_activity ['(' activity_formal_list ')']
      assertions .

R activity_locals
    = R 01 assertions
    | R 02 type_segment
    | R 03 subtype_segment
    | R 04 class_segment
    | R 05 external_segment_f_a
    | R 06 function_segment
    | R 07 activity_segment
    | R 08 interpreter_or_static function_segment
    | R 09 interpreter_or_static activity_segment
    | R 10 declare_statement
    | R 11 activity_import_statement .

R activity_invocations_part
    = 01 activity_invocation_list
    | R 02 activity_invocation_list assertions
    | R 03 activity_invocation_list format_statement_list
    | R 04 activity_invocation_list assertions
      format_statement_list .

R activity_formal_list
 = 01 activity_formal_sublist
 | 02 activity_formal_sublist ';' activity_formal_list .

R activity_formal_sublist
 = 01 activity_formal_input_or_modifiable_sublist
 | 02 'W' activity_formal_input_or_modifiable_sublist
 | R 03 'ATT' activity_formal_attribute_sublist .

R activity_formal_input_or_modifiable_sublist
 = 01 identifier_list:def_object ':' type_designator .

R activity_formal_attribute_sublist
 = 01 identifier_list:def_object ':' type_designator
 | R 02 identifier_list:def_type_or_function_or_activity
       ':' generic_designator .

R activity_import_statement
 = 01 'IMPORT' activity_import_list ('ENDIMPORT' | 'END') .

R activity_import_list
 = 01 import_identifier_list [';' activity_import_list]
 | 02 'W' import_identifier_list [';' activity_import_list] .

21.4.3. Description

description_segment
 = 01 'DESCRIPTION' description_header
       'BODY' { description_locals }
       ('END' | end_identifier)
 | R 02 'DESCRIPTION' description_header
       'BODY' { description_locals }
       description_body_invocation_part
       ('END' | end_identifier) .

description_header
 = 01 identifier:def_description
      [description_formal_lists]
 | R 02 identifier:def_description
      [description_formal_lists] assertions .

description_locals
    = R 01 assertions
    | R 02 type_segment
    | R 03 subtype_segment
    | R 04 class_segment
    | R 05 external_segment_f_a_d
    | R 06 function_segment
    | R 07 activity_segment
    | R 08 interpreter_or_static function_segment
    | R 09 interpreter_or_static activity_segment
    | R 10 description_segment
    | R 11 use_statement
    | R 12 declare_statement .

R description_body_invocation_part
    =   01 activity_invocation_list
    | R 02 activity_invocation_list assertions .

description_formal_lists
    =   01 '(' description_formal_interface_list ')'
    | R 02 '(' description_formal_attribute_list ')'
        '(' description_formal_interface_list ')'
    | R 03 '(' description_formal_attribute_list ')' .

description_formal_interface_list
    = 01 description_formal_interface_sublist
    | 02 description_formal_interface_sublist ';'
        description_formal_interface_list .

E description_formal_interface_sublist
    = R 01 'IN' description_formal_sublist
    | R 02 'OUT' description_formal_sublist
    | R 03 'INOUT' description_formal_sublist .

description_formal_sublist
    = 01 identifier_list:def_object ':' type_designator .

R description_formal_attribute_list
    = 01 description_formal_attribute_sublist
    | 02 description_formal_attribute_sublist ';'
        description_formal_attribute_list .

R description_formal_attribute_sublist
   = 01 identifier_list:def_object ':' type_designator .

21.4.4. Type, Subtype and Class

R type_segment
   = 01 'TYPE' type_header 'BODY' type_derivation
      ('END' | end_identifier)
   | R 02 'TYPE' type_header 'BODY' type_derivation
      type_locals { type_locals } ('END' | end_identifier) .

R type_derivation
   = 01 type_set_construction
    ['CARRYALL' | 'CARRY' type_carry_list
       ('ENDCARRY' | 'END')] .

R type_header
   = 01 identifier:def_type
   | R 02 identifier:def_type '(' type_formal_attributes_list ')' .

R type_locals
   = R 01 type_segment
   | R 02 subtype_segment
   | R 03 class_segment
   | R 04 ['PRIVATE'] function_segment
   | R 05 ['PRIVATE'] interpreter_or_static function_segment
   | R 06 ['PRIVATE'] activity_segment
   | R 07 ['PRIVATE'] interpreter_or_static activity_segment
   | R 08 format_statement .

R type_carry_list
   = R 01 function_identifier [',' type_carry_list]
   | R 02 activity_identifier [',' type_carry_list] .

R type_formal_attributes_list
   = 01 type_formal_attributes_sublist
   | 02 type_formal_attributes_sublist ';'
    type_formal_attributes_list .

R type_formal_attributes_sublist
   = 01 identifier_list:def_object ':' type_designator
   | R 02 identifier_list:def_type ':' class_designator .

R subtype_segment
   = 01 'SUBTYPE' subtype_header 'BODY' subtype_set_construction
      ('END' | end_identifier) .

R subtype_header
   = 01 identifier:def_type
   | R 02 identifier:def_type '(' type_formal_attributes_list ')' .

R class_segment
   = 01 'CLASS' class_header 'BODY' class_set_construction
      ('END' | end_identifier) .

R class_header
   = 01 identifier:def_class
   | R 02 identifier:def_class '(' type_formal_attributes_list ')' .

R type_set_construction
   = R 01 'ALL' identifier:def_object ':' type_designator 'WITH'
      expression_1:bool_constant ('ENDALL' | 'END')
   | R 02 '{' [constant_denotation_list] '}'
   | R 03 type_designator .

R subtype_set_construction
   = R 01 'ALL' identifier:def_object ':' type_designator 'WITH'
      expression_1:bool_constant ('ENDALL' | 'END')
   | R 02 type_designator .

R class_set_construction
   = R 01 'ALL' identifier:def_type ':' class_designator 'WITH'
      expression_1:bool_constant ('ENDALL' | 'END')
   | R 02 '{' [type_designator_list] '}' ·
   | R 03 class_designator .

R assertions
   = 01 'ASSERT' assert_expr { ',' assert_expr }
      ('ENDASSERT' | 'END') .

ER assert_expr
   = R 01 expression_1:bool .

21.4.5. Conlan

R conlan_segment
    = 01 'CONLAN' identifier:def_language 'BODY'
      ['CARRYALL' | 'CARRY' conlan_carry_list
             ('ENDCARRY' | 'END')]
      { ['PRIVATE']
        (type_segment
        | subtype_segment
        | class_segment
        | [interpreter_or_static] function_segment
        | [interpreter_or_static] activity_segment
        | description_segment)
      | external_segment_f_a_d
      | format_statement }
      ('END' | end_identifier) .

R conlan_carry_list
    = 01 type_identifier [',' conlan_carry_list]
    | 02 class_identifier [',' conlan_carry_list]
    | 03 function_identifier [',' conlan_carry_list]
    | 04 activity_identifier [',' conlan_carry_list]
    | 05 description_identifier [',' conlan_carry_list] .

21.5. Statements

21.5.1. Expression

E expression_1
    = R 01 expression_2
    | R 02 expression_1 '|' expression_2
    | R 03 expression_1 '~|' expression_2   "/ bcl /"
    | R 04 expression_1 'OR' expression_2 .   "/ bcl /"

ER expression_2
    = R 01 expression_3
    | R 02 expression_2 'XOR' expression_3   "/ bcl /"
    | R 03 expression_2 'EQV' expression_3 .   "/ bcl /"

ER expression_3
    = R 01 expression_4
    | R 02 expression_3 '&' expression_4
    | R 03 expression_3 '~&' expression_4   "/ bcl /"
    | R 04 expression_3 'AND' expression_4 .   "/ bcl /"

ER expression_4
    = R 01 expression_5
    | R 02 expression_5 '=' expression_5
    | R 03 expression_5 '~=' expression_5
    | R 04 expression_5 '<' expression_5
    | R 05 expression_5 '=<' expression_5
    | R 06 expression_5 '>=' expression_5
    | R 07 expression_5 '>' expression_5
    | R 08 expression_5 '.<' expression_5
    | R 09 expression_5 '<|' expression_5
    | R 10 expression_5 'EQ' expression_5   "/ bcl /"
    | R 11 expression_5 '~EQ' expression_5 .   "/ bcl /"

ER expression_5
    = R 01 expression_6
    | R 02 expression_5 '+' expression_6
    | R 03 expression_5 '-' expression_6 .

ER expression_6
    = R 01 expression_7
    | R 02 expression_6 '*' expression_7
    | R 03 expression_6 '/' expression_7
    | R 04 expression_6 'MOD' expression_7 .

ER expression_7
    = R 01 expression_8
    | R 02 expression_7 '↑' expression_8
    | R 03 expression_7 '%' expression_8 .   "/ bcl /"

ER expression_8
    = R 01 expression_9
    | R 02 '~' expression_9
    | R 03 '-' expression_9
    | R 04 '+' expression_9 .

ER expression_9
    = R 01 expression_10
    | R 02 expression_9 '#' expression_10 .   "/ bcl /"

ER expression_10
    = R 01 declared_identifier
    | R 02 type_designator
    | R 03 class_designator
    | R 04 unsigned_constant_denotation
    | R 05 function_invocation
    | R 06 conditional_expression
    | R 07 predicate
    | R 08 set_selection
    | R 09 '(' expression_1 ')'
    | R 10 expression_10 '[.' expression_1 '.]'   "/ bcl /"
    | R 11 expression_10 '[' dimension_list ']'   "/ bcl /"
    | R 12 expression_10 '!' string_denotation   "/ bcl /"
    | R 13 expression_10 '{' expression_1 '}'   "/ bcl /"
    | R 14 expression_10 '{' expression_1 ','
        expression_1 '}'   "/ bcl /"
    | R 15 expression_10 '{' expression_1 ',' '}'   "/ bcl /"
    | R 16 expression_10 '{' '}'   "/ bcl /"
    | R 17 argument_tag .   "/ only legal within MEANS-part /"

R predicate
    = R 01 'FORALL@' identifier:def_object ':' type_designator 'IS'
        expression_1:bool ('ENDFORALL' | 'ENDFOR' | 'END')
    | R 02 'FORSOME@' identifier:def_object ':' type_designator 'IS'
        expression_1:bool ('ENDFORSOME' | 'ENDFOR' | 'END')
    | R 03 'FORONE@' identifier:def_object ':' type_designator 'IS'
        expression_1:bool ('ENDFORONE' | 'ENDFOR' | 'END') .

R set_selection
    = 01 'THE@' identifier:def_object ':' type_designator 'WITH'
      expression_1:bool ('ENDTHE' | 'END') .

ER conditional_expression
    = R 01 'IF' if_cond_expr 'THEN' then_else_expr
        { 'ELIF' if_cond_expr 'THEN' then_else_expr }
        'ELSE' then_else_expr ('ENDIF' | 'END')
    | R 02 'CASE' case_cond_expr 'IS' case_expression_element_list
        ['ELSE' case_elem_expr] ('ENDCASE' | 'END') .

R case_expression_element_list
    = 01 case_expression_element
    | 02 case_expression_element ';' case_expression_element_list .

R case_expression_element
    = 01 constant_denotation_list ':' case_elem_expr .

ER if_cond_expr
    = R 01 expression_1:bool .

ER then_else_expr
    = R 01 expression_1 .

ER case_cond_expr
    = R 01 expression_1 .

ER case_elem_expr
    = R 01 expression_1 .

21.5.2. Operation_invocation

R function_invocation
    =   01 function_identifier
        '(' [function_actual_parameter_list] ')'
    | R 02 function_identifier .

R function_actual_parameter_list
    = 01 f_a_act_param_expr
    | 02 f_a_act_param_expr ',' function_actual_parameter_list .

ER f_a_act_param_expr
    = R 01 expression_1
    | R 02 activity_identifier .   "/ actual generic parameter /"

E activity_invocation
    =   01 simple_activity_invocation
    | R 02 conditional_activity_invocation
    | R 03 repeated_activity_invocation .

E simple_activity_invocation
    = R 01 activity_identifier
       '(' [activity_actual_parameter_list] ')'
    | R 02 expression_1 '.=' expression_1   "/ bcl /"
    | R 03 expression_1 ':=' expression_1   "/ bcl /"
    | R 04 expression_1 '<-' expression_1 .   "/ bcl /"

R activity_actual_parameter_list
    = 01 f_a_act_param_expr
    | 02 f_a_act_param_expr ',' activity_actual_parameter_list .

 activity_invocation_list
    = 01 activity_invocation [',' activity_invocation_list] .

ER conditional_activity_invocation
    = R 01 'IF' if_cond_expr 'THEN' activity_invocation_list
       { 'ELIF' if_cond_expr 'THEN' activity_invocation_list }
       ['ELSE' activity_invocation_list] ('ENDIF' | 'END')
    | R 02 'CASE' case_cond_expr 'IS' case_activity_element_list
       ['ELSE' activity_invocation_list]
       ('ENDCASE' | 'END') .

R case_activity_element_list
    = 01 case_activity_element
    | R 02 case_activity_element ';' case_activity_element_list .

R case_activity_element
    = 01 constant_denotation_list ':' [activity_invocation_list] .

R repeated_activity_invocation
    = R 01 'OVER' identifier:def_object 'FROM' over_expr
       ['STEP' over_expr] 'TO' over_expr
       'REPEAT' activity_invocation_list
       ('ENDOVER' | 'END')
    | R 02 'OVER' identifier:def_object ':' type_set_construction
       'REPEAT' activity_invocation_list
       ('ENDOVER' | 'END') .

ER over_expr
    = R 01 expression_1:int_constant .

21.5.3. Declare and Use

R declare_statement

    = 01 'DECLARE' declaration_list ('ENDDECLARE' | 'END') .

R declaration_list

    = 01 declaration

    | 02 declaration ';' declaration_list .

R declaration

    =   01 identifier_list:def_object ':' type_designator

    | R 02 identifier_list:def_object ':' type_designator

        '=' declare_expr .

ER declare_expr

    = R 01 expression_1:constant_or_car_type .

R use_statement

    = 01 'USE' use_list ('ENDUSE' | 'END') .

R use_list

    = 01 use

    | 02 use ';' use_list .

R use

    = 01 instantiation_list ':' description_designator .

R instantiation_list

    = 01 instantiation

    | 02 instantiation ',' instantiation_list .

R instantiation

    = 01 identifier_array_use

      ['(' description_actual_interface_list ')'] .

R identifier_array_use

    =   01 identifier:def_instance

    | R 02 identifier:def_instance use_range_list .

R use_range_list

    = 01 '[' use_expression_range_list ']' .

R use_expression_range_list
    = 01 use_expression_range
    | R 02 use_expression_range
       ';' use_expression_range_list .

R use_expression_range
    = 01 use_expr ':' use_expr .

ER use_expr
    = R 01 expression_1:int_constant .

R description_actual_interface_list
    = 01 [descr_act_interface_expr]
    | R 02 [descr_act_interface_expr] ','
       description_actual_interface_list .

ER descr_act_interface_expr
    = R 01 expression_1 .

R description_designator
    = 01 description_identifier
    | R 02 description_identifier
       '(' description_actual_attribute_list ')' .

R description_actual_attribute_list
    = 01 descr_act_att_expr
    | R 02 descr_act_att_expr ','
       description_actual_attribute_list .

ER descr_act_att_expr
    = R 01 expression_1:constant .

21.5.4. Syntax Modification

R format_statement_list
    = 01 format_statement { format_statement } .

R format_statement
    = 01 ['DEFERRED@'] 'FORMAT@'
       syntax_directive { syntax_directive }
       ('END' | 'ENDFORMAT') .

R syntax_directive
   = 01 'EXTEND' alternative_extension
   | 02 'REMOVE' production_or_alternative_identifier
     { ',' production_or_alternative_identifier } .

R production_or_alternative_identifier
   = 01 identifier
   | 02 identifier '.' alternative_number .

R alternative_number
   = 01 decimal_denotation .

R alternative_extension
   = 01 identifier '.' alternative_number [restrictions]
     '=' ['R'] alternative_text { alternative_text }
     [means_part]
   | 02 identifier '.' alternative_number means_part .

R means_part
   = R 01 'MEANS' function_invocation
   | R 02 'MEANS' '(' expression_1 ')'
   | R 03 'MEANS' set_selection
   | R 04 'MEANS' activity_invocation
   | R 05 'MEANS' meaning .

R meaning
   = 01 '"/"' { character } '"/"' .

R argument_tag
   = R 01 '@' decimal_denotation
   | R 02 '@' identifier '.' decimal_denotation
     '.' decimal_denotation .

R alternative_list
   = 01 alternative_text { alternative_text }
     { '|' alternative_text { alternative_text } } .

R alternative_text
   = 01 identifier [':' attribute_tag]
   | 02 terminal_symbol
   | 03 '[' alternative_list ']'
   | 04 '{' alternative_list '}'
   | 05 '(' alternative_list ')' .

R attribute_tag
   = 01 identifier .

R terminal_symbol
   = 01 string_denotation .

R restrictions
   = 01 'E'
   | 02 'R'
   | 03 'E' 'R'
   | 04 'R' 'E' .

ENDSYNTAX

Index

Subtypes 7

T@ 107, 109
Tail@ 113
Terminal 139
Terminal@ 138
THE@ 23, 31, 48
THEN 23
TO 23, 49
Toolmaker 5
Transfer 141
Transpose 124
Tuple@ 59
Tuplize@ 113
Type 7, 23, 28, 31, 38, 41, 42, 44
Type checking 7, 9
Type definition segment 7
Type derivation 7
Type designator 7, 9
Type family 7
Type_designator 50
Type_part@ 131
Tytuple 113

Univ@ 48, 62
UNTIL 23
USE 23, 31, 39, 50
User 5

Val 137, 138, 139, 141
Val_type 112
Value 59, 112
Variable 141
Variable@ 139
Vpart@ 121
Vsize@ 122

W 35, 36
WITH 23, 48

Xor 111

{ 48

| 23, 61, 63

} 48

~ 23, 61, 63
~& 112
~= 23, 61, 62, 63, 64
~| 111